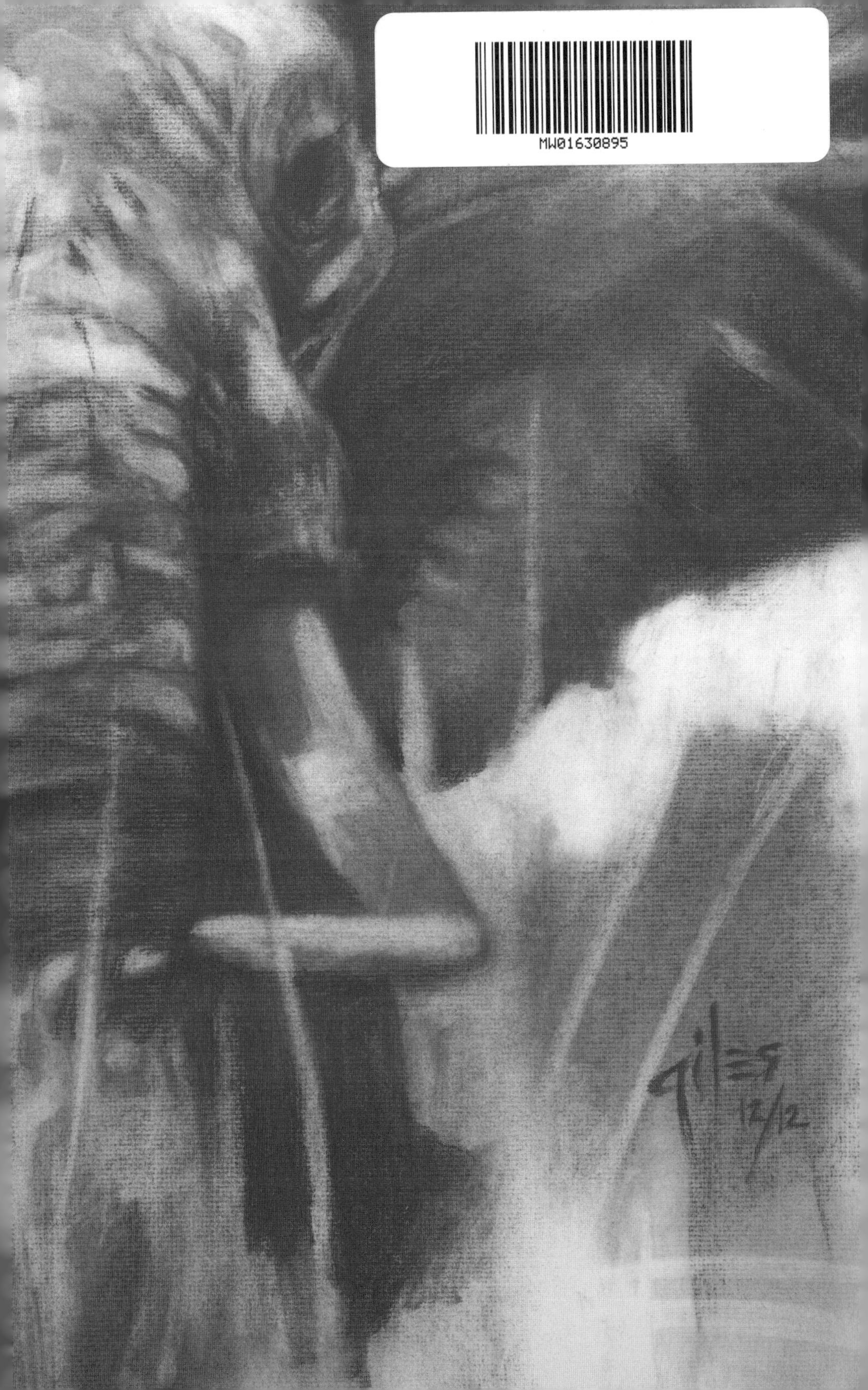

MW01630895
giles
12/12

RISE, KILL & EAT

RISE, KILL & EAT

A Theology of Hunting from Genesis to Revelation

For Am: Bob,
Best Wishes!

Doug Giles

Doug 10-29-15

LIBERTY ALLIANCE
DALLAS, GEORGIA

RISE, KILL & EAT

A Theology of Hunting from Genesis to Revelation

by Doug Giles

Published by:

Liberty Alliance
147 Ponderosa Trail
Dallas, GA 30132

Jacket design by: David Bugnon of Mobopolis.com
Original artwork by Doug Giles · RiseKillandEat.com
Jacket photo of Doug Giles by Michael O'Fallon

ISBN: 978-1-4951-0934-8

Printed in the United States of America.

In Dedication

This book is dedicated to the hunter, angler and trapper who's tired of listening to the blather from the anti-hunting bunny lovers that disparage the phenomenal positive impact our pursuits have on true conservation.

Rise, kill and eat my friends.

Rise, kill and eat.

The Gut Pile

Foreword

Hunting is one of the last, perfect acts of environmental upgrade available to mankind. Not only does this time honored sport provide untold metric tons of pure, ultra-nutritious, renewable protein to the dinner tables of tens of millions of families across America every year as we balance the herds and monitor the good mother earth, but this exciting hunting challenge is the last hope for quality air, soil and water for planet earth.

After all, it has been the trillions of dollars generated for more than 100 years by hunting families that have secured, rehabilitated, upgraded, safeguarded and perfected those sacred grounds and waterways from which our life force environment produces these essences of quality of life. You want environmental quality; buy a hunting license, a fishing license and a trapping license.

In 2014 and beyond, the only thing more important for quality of life in America than killing many, many deer each fall, is killing the scourge of political correctness that has festered the soulless cult of denial so rampant in the land. We need to look no further than the existence of the animal rights scam as the ultimate example of the dumbing down of America. The sheer brain-dead ignorance one must cultivate, nurture and maniacally protect in order to reduce living, breathing, precious flesh and blood wildlife to the level of a cartoon character says all that needs to be said for this pathetic cult of scammers.

In this raging culture war against the denial zombies, I am proud to stand shoulder-to-shoulder, bloody venison haunch to bloody venison haunch with my American warrior BloodBrother, Doug Giles.

Doug has always fought the good fight with his razor sharp samurai sword of self-evident truth, logic, commonsense, science and The American Way.

> In this raging culture war against the denial zombies, I am proud to stand shoulder-to-shoulder, bloody venison haunch to bloody venison haunch with my American warrior BloodBrother, Doug Giles.

In his killer new book ***RISE, KILL & EAT: A Theology of Hunting From Genesis to Revelation*** Doug carries on with his courageous war against the lunatic fringe who dare recommend Bambi solutions to the annual production of edible wildlife. Doug lives the good hunt life, and in this book wallows boldly in irrefutable evidence and scientific reality to conclusively trounce the bizarre nonsense of hands-off, tax torching, government "sharpshooter", renewable wildlife damage control instead of the time honored win-win of American sporters venison Thanksgiving quality control.

If you truly want to know how America could be so stupid as to turn over the Last Best Place to a Chicago community organizer scam artist and his gunrunning attorney general, just watch pathetic anti-hunters twist themselves into a trance in their feeble attempt to convince you venison isn't authorized food.

I am celebrating the release of Doug's new book by taking a bunch of young boys and girls along with a bunch of American military warriors and their families on numerous hunting trips this spring for wild turkeys, of which there are more today than when Columbus first landed here, and on our annual wild pig slaughter from helicopters with machineguns. As we do so, we save massive tax dollars, save family farms and ranches, save the environment, save wildlife, create jobs, generate gobs of revenues and feed homeless shelters and soup kitchens with many tons of the most delicious, organic, pure pork known to man.

And then there are the zombies that would ban it. I'm with Doug Giles.

–Ted Nugent

giles
1/09

Introduction

For the last ten years I've been a weekly contributor for one of the nation's largest news portals, Townhall.com. For those who've read my screeds via TownHall.com or via my own website, ClashDaily.com, you know that I'm an unapologetic cheerleader for hunting. It's not the only thing I write about, but OMG when I do, boy … do I gush like a schoolgirl.

However, not everyone is cool with hunting like the like the planet's population used to be since the dawn of man. Hunters are becoming a rare breed in this increasingly wussified, paranormal culture of political correctness. Thanks to Disney movies, hunting nowadays is about as popular as a bacon sandwich is to a Shi'ite Muslim.

Yep, that which used to be a given within our American milieu is barely tolerated by the intolerant "tolerant" amongst us. If you're a hunter, or a non-hunter who gets the role of hunting for the conservation of both land and species, then you're looked upon by the ubiquitous bunny lovers with a glare that is one part bewilderment and one part disdain.

So … why do the anti-hunters and those who're punch drunk with their propaganda hate hunting and hunters so much? Heck, if I know. But I'm pretty certain it has not as much to do with actually killing and eating animals as it does with owning firearms. Sure the PETA freaks will caterwaul that it's all about them not digging us putting the bam to Bambi, but if you follow the money you'll probably find out that they're funded by a Leftist agenda that has a bigger game plan in play.

The control freaks, you see, aren't comfortable when the people they are trying to oppress own weapons, so they have to whiz on activities which afford these serfs the skill and the tools to say, "Back the blank off." But that's a topic for another book. Matter of fact, I covered that topic in my last book, The Sandy Hook Massacre: When Seconds Count, Police Are Minutes Away. ***What a coincidence.***

As you'll quickly notice as you plow on, I'm pretty much cool with the anti-hunter's derision. Honestly, I'd miss it if I weren't ticking these people off on a regular basis. They're irrational, fueled by emotion and bereft of facts and thus, I feel it is my job to tweak 'em every chance I get with the beneficial reality of hunting. Call me a gadfly.

The group that I do not get, who should know better, who're becoming increasingly anti-hunting at the speed of sound are … Christians, or at least those who call themselves Christians. You'd think that Christians would have as their guide the Scripture framing their life's glide path but alas … nah. The reason being? Well, it's primarily predicated upon Christians not reading the Bible, in its entirety, but rather getting their worldview from some metrosexual pastor who takes his cue from Shakira, or some hipster twit that has a fawn for a pet, or some commie running their Poli-Sci class at Tallahassee Junior College, or some lesbian misandrist who's decided she's going to rail against everything Rosie O'Donnell doesn't do. In my humble opinion, it's a shame and a sin that Christians look to Justin Bieber more than Jeremiah for life's answers.

I can't begin to count the multitudinous times I have heard from the squeamish brethren, stoked on feelings versus facts, who tell me that Jesus is mad at me, and that I'm the bad guy, for simply carrying out the covenant blessing of being a hunter.

> I can't begin to count the multitudinous times I have heard from the squeamish brethren, stoked on feelings versus facts, who tell me that Jesus is mad at me, and that I'm the bad guy, for simply carrying out the covenant blessing of being a hunter.

However, if (and that's a big if), if the Christian did look to Scripture and pay particular attention to the passages within the Bible that address the topic of hunting, then they'll walk away thinking not only is hunting animals tolerated but it is endorsed by God. And that's exactly what this little book is about: to prove that God, from Genesis to Revelation, is extremely cool with hunters and hunting. I'll go out on a biblical limb and claim right off the bat that you cannot show me, through the balance of the Bible, that the God of the Scripture is against the killing and the grilling of the animals he created. To this carnivore it is simple: if God did not want us to eat animals then he would have not made them out of meat.

As stated, this books sole intent is to showcase, through both the Old Testament and the New, what the Scriptures say about hunting, so that when you, the hunter, get around the whiners screaming foul when it comes to hunting, you can stand firm on the Verbum Dei, feel proud, and say in regards to this important activity, "Hey, leave me alone. I'm simply doing the Lord's work."

My method going forward is to take the Christian Bible, as a piece of literature, and simply report what I find it says about hunters, hunting and meat consumption. What you're going to find is that there is not a ton of passages within the Bible that directly address hunting and hunters but the parts that do are pro-hunting.

Doug Giles
Miami, Florida
May 2014

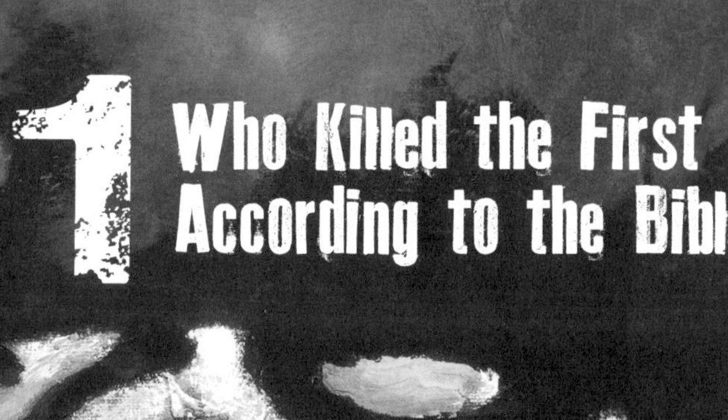

1 Who Killed the First Animal According to the Bible?

Who Killed the First Animal According to the Bible?

No doubt, I'm sure some of you are thinking that it probably was Satan or someone closely connected to him like that godless tramp Jezebel, or possibly an idiotic idolater? Or, I know, it was that Gadarene demoniac freak, in the Gospel of Mark, who was running around naked in that graveyard cutting himself with rocks! Yep, it's got to be him. That fool would have killed a cuddly rabbit with no problemo whatsoever. I mean, he did cause a herd of pigs to plunge over a cliff to their doom. No. I'm sorry. The demoniac did not cause that to occur; but, rather, Jesus was the one who okayed that mass slaughter of two thousand swine (Mark 5:1-13) by directing the exorcised demons into a herd of Wilburs. But I digress. Back to hunting.

So, who felled the first animal according the Bible? Well, I hate to break it to you but it was neither el Diablo, Jezebel, nor the Gadarene demoniac that slayed the first beast.

No, the first person within the word of God, whom Scripture states drew first blood was ... wait for it ... you ain't gonna believe this ... hold on ... are you sitting down? Here it comes ... it ... was ... (drum roll please) ... none other than God, himself.

Now, before you think I'm several ounces short of a Big Gulp, remember our standard is the Bible; and the first reference I can find within this particular book of an animal getting off'ed is right here peeps...

RISE, KILL & EAT

"Unto Adam also and to his wife did the LORD God make coats of skins, and clothed them." – Genesis 3:21

Check it out: the first animal to die, according to Scripture, was, by inference, via the hand of God.

At least I'm guessing that it was God.

"Unto Adam also and to his wife did the LORD God make coats of skins, and clothed them."

Genesis 3:21

I mean, it seems to me pretty clear from the aforementioned text that, after Adam and Eve had sinned, Yahweh made for them coats made of skins. Please note that the verse did not say he made them onesies out of wool or cardigans built of cashmere. It says, the Lord God made coats out of skin. Skin, folks. Skin. S-K-I-N, skin.

Now, y'all help me here because I'm not the smartest dude schlepping this pebble, but the last time I checked, when you skinned an animal it was usually dead or it died a horrible death soon after. Surely, God wouldn't have skinned an animal alive, would he? Nah. That would have been really cruel, eh? So, I'm a guessin' that Jehovah put the animal down before he pulled its skin off and made Adam and Eve some haute couture.

Yep, the bible doesn't say that God went to Macy's to grab some Ralph Lauren, or that God found some fresh roadkill and stripped their nasty hides, so I assume that some critter had to take one for the team in order to clothe our rebellious first parents – and that animal was slain by the hand of God.

Who else could/would have done it? Surely, not the metrosexual Adam who was afraid of snakes. And why, if someone else killed the critter, does the book of Genesis say the LORD God provided the skins ***in which Adam and Eve were donned?***

Look, if any of you sages out there in biblical-interpretation land have any other conclusion on what it means when the Bible says, "Unto Adam also and to his wife did the LORD God make coats of skins, and clothed them," then please … thrill me with it. Because, from an unfiltered read of this passage, this redneck understands this to mean that God did-in the first critter in order to provide some leather to wear for our fallen folks.

Which brings up a couple of other interesting points.

First off, because this event took place prior to the flood, the meat was wasted because no meat was consumed until after the Noahic flood (see Genesis 9:1-3). OMG, what will the bunny lovers do with that revelation?

Secondly, I don't know what animal was utilized for making Adam and Eve some ready-to-wear (probably a leopard, I mean that's what I would have used) but it is clear that God, who could have used cotton or bark or grass skirts to clothe these two knuckleheads, chose instead to use leather. Rock-n-Roll. God's not only the initial one to put the first animal to rest, but he is also a fashion designer that used animal skins to clothe his creation.

So, my little children who love to hunt, what do we learn from this little Bible study? Succinctly, it is this: the next time your nasally neighbor gives you grief about hunting an animal and/

or wearing leather simply tell the naysayers that you're "following the lead of our Father, which art in heaven, hallowed be His name."

Was Noah's Ark One Big, Floating, Game Ranch?

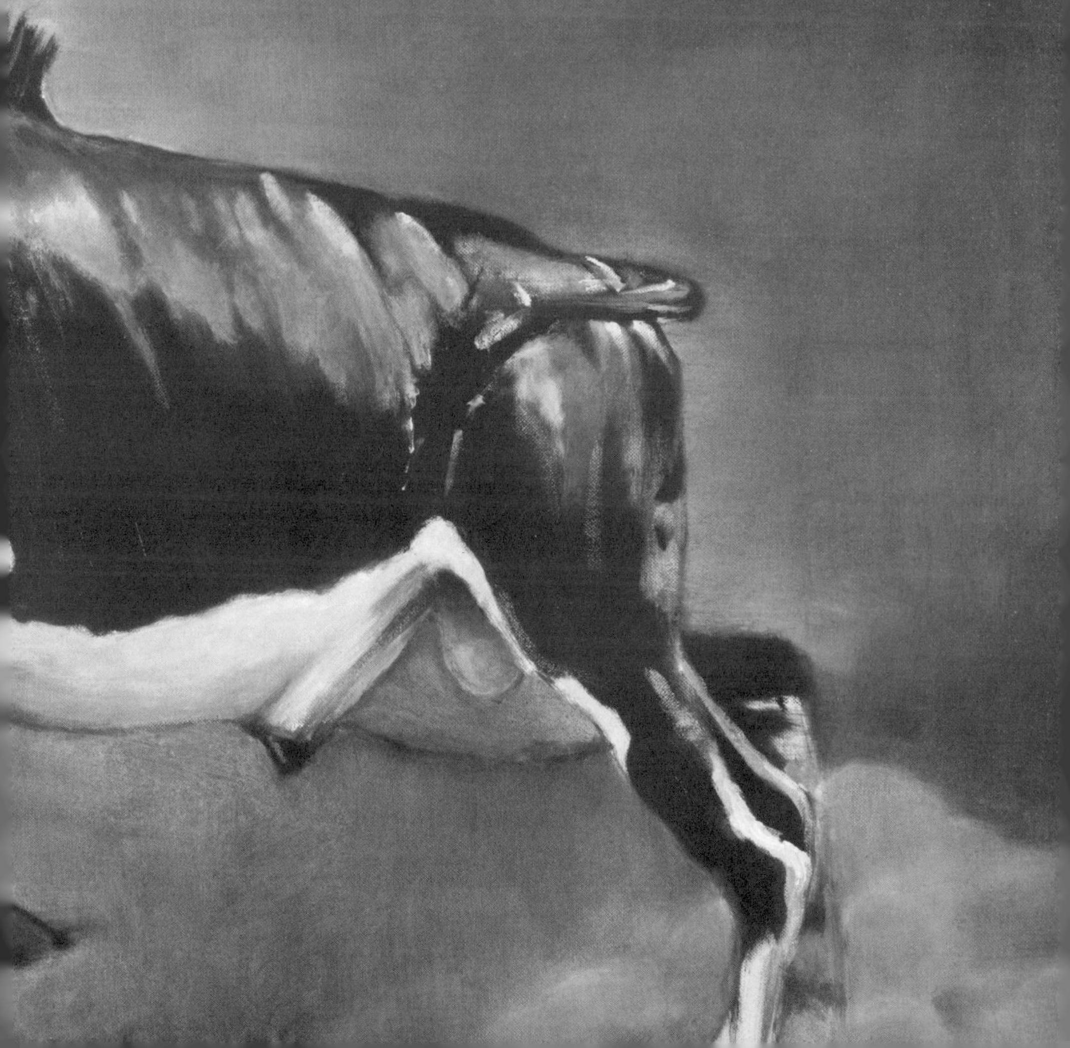

Was Noah's Ark One Big, Floating, Game Ranch?

And God blessed Noah and his sons and said to them, "Be fruitful and multiply, and fill the earth. The fear of you and the terror of you will be on every beast of the earth and on every bird of the sky; with everything that creeps on the ground, and all the fish of the sea, into your hand they are given. Every moving thing that is alive shall be food for you; I give all to you, as [I gave] the green plant." -- Genesis 9:1-3

Boy, if there ever was a chunk of scripture that the vegetarians wished wasn't in the Scripture, its gotta be this one. Yep, in these three verses God green lights the hunting, killing and eating of animals, birds, iguanas and fish. A Cyclops can see that.

Essentially, God said in effect unto Noah and his posterity that, "everything that walks, crawls or flies ... dies." Yes, "everything that you wish to eat Noah, go ahead and whack it and stack it." (Author's paraphrase).

Question: Does my brutish paraphrase capture the gist of that text? It does for me. Seems to me like a pretty plain and simple, easy to read, hard to misinterpret, instruction that someone with three teeth and an IQ of 50 could scan and understand.

Which makes me wonder a wee bit whether or not all those animals God saved from the flood he actually intended to be turned into chicken fried steak? Boy, that'll jack with your view of sweet Jesus, eh? It appears as if God had more in store for this elaborate zoo that Noah compiled.

Think about it. Could that endearing Sunday school story of Noah's Ark saving two animals of every type really be about a big floating game ranch that the sovereign God pre-arranged for Noah's tribe to hunt and grub once the floodwaters subsided? Sure looks suspicious to me. Check it out: if God is omniscient, and I believe that he is, then he obviously knew he was going to update mankind's menu to include venison, so I've got to conclude he knew these animals were going to be salt and peppered one day soon. Very soon.

Could that endearing Sunday school story of Noah's Ark saving two animals of every type really be about a big floating game ranch that the sovereign God pre-arranged for Noah's tribe to hunt and grub once the floodwaters subsided?

Imagine that: God Almighty was the first game rancher, who conserved species, not for the purpose of petting them in a menagerie, but rather for the express purpose of consuming them with fava beans and a nice Chianti.

Finally, I would be remiss if I didn't underscore a couple more nuggets tucked in those three texts, and I hate to be "remiss", whatever that is, because it sounds bad, or at least pretty disappointing.

Please note:

Nugget #1: Pursuing game and eating the game's back-straps or the fish's fresh filets is a "blessing" that God gave to humanity. Let me say that again ... it ... is ... a ... blessing.

For those not hip to what a blessing is, in biblical terms a blessing is a good thing. For a young man that likes blonds it would be like God sending him a wife who looked like Heidi Klum and had the heart of Mother Teresa. For brunette fanciers it would be like netting a Salma Hayek with the heart of a saint. Cowabunga. Score. Hunting, therefore, is not a "necessary evil" that the anti-hunters have made it out to be, but rather a biblical blessing God bestowed unto man. At least that's what the Bible says...

Nugget #2: Animals are to fear man. Why? Well, we're going to eat them, that's one solid reason for their trepidation. Indeed, from the rainbow forward animals understood that the biped who's currently crawling towards them in camouflage, sporting a Winchester Model 70 in 30/06, is out to turn them into roast beef. To level the playing field Jehovah gave animals heightened sensibilities and four legs to haul ass on so that both men and animals could maintain their respective numbers.

3 Nimrod, A Mighty Hunter Before the LORD

Freedom
giles

Nimrod, A Mighty Hunter Before the LORD

Cush was the father of Nimrod, who became a mighty warrior on the earth. He was a mighty hunter before the Lord; that is why it is said, "Like Nimrod, a mighty hunter before the Lord." – Genesis 10:9

As stated at the outset of this amazing tome about hunting, I'm going to focus on what the Bible says about hunting and hunters and not what other sources say about hunting and hunters. Capice?

As I cued up to pen this chapter on Nimrod, I couldn't help from harkening back to all the bad crap I heard about this ancient hunter. From what I got via my discipleship in church, you'd a thought Nimrod was Satan's horrible little stepbrother who lived to pull the legs off frogs and watch Swamp People marathons.

This cat was pitched to me as one of the dastardliest dawgs of the ancient world, and the lame anti-hunters attempted to use this man and his supposed checkered past as a dissuasive example to get me to shy away from hunting because it could lead me away from the Lord to build a rebellious city of decadence, like … like … like … Babylon!

As a new Christian and a hunter, I sat slack-jawed as I listened to these horror stories about Nimrod. I thought, "Man, I don't want to build a wicked city that Jesus hates like Nimrod the great hunter did, so I'd better give up hunting!" Derrrr. I know … no one ever accused me of being the sharpest knife in the drawer.

The only problem I had with my effeminate Christian leaders' take on old Nimrod was, when they started whizzing on him, they could never cite biblical sources, it was always the extra-biblical stuff that pitched Nimrod as some cloven hoofed amalgamation of Ted Nugent, Donald Trump and Howard Stern. Yea, a veritable trifecta of greed, vice and hunting that every young, sweet, Christian male should eschew.

The only problem they had getting me to disparage hunting was they had no scriptural proof to back up their opinions/conclusions regarding my godly pursuit.

So, when I started scrabbling together what I know about the Bible and hunting for this project, I Googled "Nimrod and the Bible" just to make certain there wasn't a huge chunk of scripture I'd overlooked many moons ago that actually BBQ'ed Nimrod and hunting. All I got were these four results where Mr. Nimrod is even mentioned! Only four. Like in: one, two, three, four. And here they are …

> "They will shepherd the land of Assyria with the sword, the land of Nimrod at its entrances; And He will deliver us from the Assyrian When he attacks our land And when he tramples our territory." – Micah 5: 6
>
> "Cush became the father of Nimrod; he began to be a mighty one in the earth." – 1 Chron.1: 10
>
> "Now Cush became the father of Nimrod; he became a mighty one on the earth. He was a mighty hunter be-

> fore the LORD; therefore it is said, "Like Nimrod a mighty hunter before the LORD. -- *Genesis 10: 8, 9*

Did you notice what is absent from the four, the only four, times Nimrod is mentioned in the scripture? There's nothing about him being nasty and demonic, or that God was really ticked at him, or that hunting caused him to become a rebel freak. There's nothing like that and much to the opposite especially if you read real s-l-o-w-l-y the passages in Genesis chapter 10.

Question: Don't you think if Nimrod were a lowdown, dirty scallywag that God would have had it written up? I mean, he didn't spare pointing out his friends and foes foibles when they got out in left field doing some anti-biblical, whacked stuff did he? Of course not. He's God, what are they going to do? Sue him? Herein lies the debacle for the Nimrod disparagers; there's nothing about Nimrod except that he was an awesome hunter before the Lord.

Some folks have pointed out to me that Nimrod's name means "rebel" and I'm like ... so? It still doesn't mean that hunting is wrong. Geez, folks. My name Douglas means: "black water". What does that mean? That I'm evil water? Or, that my favorite song has to be the Doobie Brother's #1 hit off their 1975 album, *What Were Once Vices Are Now Habits*?

Look, Nimrod's name could mean "Satan's scrotum" and it still doesn't mean that hunting is evil. Maybe his parents were naming him that, but not the activity of hunting. Get a grip folks. Jesus' great, great, great granny Rahab's name means, "large, broad" -- does that mean that she was destined to have a big booty? Not necessarily, and anyway, since the advent of JLo and Kim Kardashian, big bottom girls are en vogue *and, thus,*

Rahab's name would not be a negative thing but a very positive nomenclature to fly by according to today's trends. Fat bottom girls, you make the rockin' world go 'round.

Another thing that my friends have pointed out to me is the phrase mighty hunter "before the Lord" actually means "in God's face." As if Nimrod was defiantly rubbing God's nose in the fact that he was putting the bam to Bambi. It was as if Nimrod was like, "Hey, God. You see that deer over there eating that farmer's carrots? Yeah, him. He doesn't know I've got a bead on him. He doesn't know I'm about to let the air out of him. Boom! I shot him, God! What are you going to do about it?"

Look, I'm no Hebrew scholar and I graduated from my undergrad studies with a solid 2.1, but I've gotta wonder if that phrase "before the Lord" actually means "rebelliously in God's face", because it is the same phrase that is used of King David when he danced before God in worship.

Check it out … And David was dancing before the LORD with all his might, and David was wearing a linen ephod. -- 2 Samuel 6:14

Now, help me here, Bible experts: does the above passage carry the same negative connotation that you purport the Nimrod text carries because, from an abecedarian's read of things, it sounds like the exact same stuff to moi.

Was David involved in rebel dancing? Was God ticked at David? Huh?

Now, for clarification, let me state that for all I know or care, Nimrod could have been bat-crap, crazy evil and he could have intentionally built a big ol' wicked city, or cities, that make Vegas look like a prudish, Amish hamlet. In addition, he could have partied so hard he made Lindsay Lohan look like a penitent nun. But, you know what? That doesn't mean hunting is dreadful. According to that dog-tired line of reasoning this is true:

> Nimrod was a Mighty Hunter
> Nimrod built cities
> These cities became evil
> *Therefore, hunting is evil.*

And if that's true than so is this:

> God is Love
> Love is blind
> Stevie Wonder is blind
> *Therefore, Stevie Wonder is God.*

Look, I'll grant you that, indeed, the cities he developed eventually went south; but that had nothing to do with hunting anymore than some American cities' degeneracy can be traced back to those principalities' founders' loving to hunt muskrats with muskets.

Nimrod was a Mighty Hunter
Nimrod built cities
These cities became evil
Therefore, hunting is evil.
And if that's true than so is this:
God is Love
Love is blind
Stevie Wonder is blind
Therefore, Stevie Wonder is God.

Just for fun, and proof, here are several major interpretations of the infamous Nimrod passage in Genesis 10: 9 …

> *New International Version* (©2011): He was a mighty hunter before the LORD; that is why it is said, "Like Nimrod, a

mighty hunter before the LORD."

New Living Translation (©2007): Since he was the greatest hunter in the world, his name became proverbial. People would say, "This man is like Nimrod, the greatest hunter in the world."

English Standard Version (©2001): He was a mighty hunter before the LORD. Therefore it is said, "Like Nimrod a mighty hunter before the LORD."

New American Standard Bible (©1995): He was a mighty hunter before the LORD; therefore it is said, "Like Nimrod a mighty hunter before the LORD."

King James Bible (Cambridge Ed.): He was a mighty hunter before the LORD: wherefore it is said, Even as Nimrod the mighty hunter before the LORD.

GOD'S WORD® Translation (©1995): He was a mighty hunter whom the LORD blessed. That's why people used to say, "[He's] like Nimrod, a mighty hunter whom the LORD blessed."

King James 2000 Bible (©2003): He was a mighty hunter before the LORD: therefore it is said, Even as Nimrod the mighty hunter before the LORD.

Dhouy Rheames Translation: And he was a stout hunter before the Lord. Hence came a proverb: Even as Nemrod the stout hunter before the Lord.

Young's Literal Translation: He hath begun to be a hero in the land; he hath been a hero in hunting before Jehovah;

therefore it is said, 'As Nimrod the hero in hunting before Jehovah.'

Question: Did any of them remotely sound like God and the biblical interpreters giving off the vibe that hunting is a sin?

Answer: Uh, no.

I rest my case...

Take Your Bow and Hunt Me Down Some Wild Game

Take Your Bow and Hunt Me Down Some Wild Game

Now it came about, when Isaac was old and his eyes were too dim to see, that he called his older son Esau and said to him, "My son." And he said to him, "Here I am." Isaac said, "Behold now, I am old [and] I do not know the day of my death. Now then, please take your gear, your quiver and your bow, and go out to the field and hunt game for me; and prepare a savory dish for me such as I love, and bring it to me that I may eat, so that my soul may bless you before I die."

Rebekah was listening while Isaac spoke to his son Esau. So when Esau went to the field to hunt for game to bring [home], Rebekah said to her son Jacob, "Behold, I heard your father speak to your brother Esau, saying, Bring me [some] game and prepare a savory dish for me, that I may eat, and bless you in the presence of the LORD before my death."

– Genesis 27:1-5

The next direct reference to hunters and hunting we come to in the Scripture is the controversial character named Esau. Before we get into dissecting the texts that surround this notorious gent, let's check out Esau's pop, Isaac.

Isaac is one of the three patriarchs of the Israelites. Yes, he's a biggee. Or, a "power hitter," for some of you baseball fans. The Jews refer to Abraham, Isaac and Jacob as the "covenant fathers", the veritable visible CEO's of their religious identity as constituted people under Jehovah's governance.

For those who can read and have read the Bible you know that, though not perfect like Jesus, the covenant fathers were quite legit. They weren't spurious, lip-service rendering, backslidden Baptists, who, in spite of their foibles, stayed on course following the Unseen God.

Yep, these gents weren't perfect, but they were examples of faith and devotion. When they were wrong, God called them out, kick their butts in some form or fashion, and they re-aligned with a soft heart towards his holy commands. Indeed, if and when they got out of sorts with Yahweh, he let them know it via hook or crook. God was not afraid of calling them out on their nonsense if it offended him and his commands.

No doubt some of you are thinking, "And your point is?"

Well, my point is this: Isaac, the covenant father, one of the three to which both Jews and Christians look to as a father of their faith, was completely cool with hunting and preferred venison (wild game) to the domesticated stuff. And you know what? God didn't rebuke him for it. Yep, the Lord God didn't send a prophet or a plague to chastise him for his love of his son's hunting or his eating of a shot and killed wild beast's roasted back straps, that's what.

Most numb nuts today think that truly spiritual people are vapid, airy fairy vegans who wear skinny jeans and a scarf, eat tofu, do group hugs and conduct Bible studies in Starbucks over no foam, skinny milk, hazelnut macchiatos because it is oh, so trendy.

Now, if hunting was a sin, or a borderline questionable activity, do you think this gentleman, this patriarch of the faith, would want to have as one of the last things he did, something that's going to anger the God he's about to meet? I. Think. Not.

But the Bible paints a very different picture than the emasculated image some effeminate moron has painted of our holy forbears; and one that I dig the most is right here: Isaac loved food that was hunted. Meditate on that for a while, anti-hunting Nancy boys.

Matter of fact, when Isaac was about to take the big dirt nap, the adios snooze, the eternal siesta, his last request was not to have one more round of kum-ba-yah with Todd the quasi-male worship leader; but rather for his oldest boy to go out into the woods and shoot and kill him some tasty grub.

Now, if hunting was a sin, or a borderline questionable activity, do you think this gentleman, this patriarch of the faith, would want to have as one of the last things he did, something that's going to anger the God he's about to meet? I. Think. Not.

Check it out: not only was his last request a meal his son hunted down, but it was also to be a part of the holy ceremony that conferred unto his firstborn the covenantal blessings stemming from Abraham and Isaac. The hunt and the meal were sacred. When's the last time your church's "special blessings" night was centered on the hunting and the eating of a wild beast, before you prayed for someone's blessing?

I'll tell you when that last time was: never. However, it was a part of this true man of God's most hallowed event. For those who know this narrative, you're well aware of Rebekah and Jacob's elaborate scheme to steal the birthright that belonged to Esau, Isaac's firstborn son.

Genesis 27: 5: Now Rebekah was listening as Isaac spoke to his son Esau. When Esau left for the open country to hunt game and bring it back, Rebekah said to her son Jacob, "Look, I overheard your father say to your brother Esau, Bring me some game and prepare me some tasty food to eat, so that I may give you my blessing in the presence of the Lord before I die.' Now, my son, listen carefully and do what I tell you: Go out to the flock and bring me two choice young goats, so I can prepare some tasty food for your father, just the way he likes it. Then take it to your father to eat, so that he may give you his blessing before he dies. Jacob said to Rebekah his mother, "But my brother Esau is a hairy man while I have smooth skin. What if my father touches me? I would appear to be tricking him and would bring down a curse on myself rather than a blessing." His mother said to him, "My son, let the curse fall on me. Just do what I say; go and get them for me. So he went and got them and brought them to his mother, and she prepared some tasty food, just the way his father liked it. Then Rebekah took the best clothes of Esau her older son, which she had in the house, and put them on her younger son Jacob. She also covered his hands and the smooth part of his neck with the goatskins. Then she handed to her son Jacob the tasty food and the bread she had made.

Let's break this deception down: While Esau was out hunting, Rebekah had their deceptive younger son, Jacob, slaughter a couple of their young domesticated goats and use their hides as gloves so he could masquerade as his hairy, older brother Esau. I know … pretty weird, eh? After Jake got his Halloween costume on, he grabbed the goat stew and went in to lie to his old man to get his godly blessing. This too is pretty jacked up.

Continuing in Genesis 27:18: He [Jacob] went to his father and said, "My father." "Yes, my son," he answered. "Who is it?" Jacob said to his father, "I am Esau your firstborn. I have done as you told me. Please sit up and eat some of my game, so that you may give me your blessing. Isaac asked his son, "How did you find it so quickly, my son?" "The Lord your God gave me success," he replied.

All right, let's check this out. Isaac asks of Jacob, thinking that he's his boy Esau who just went out hunting, "How did you find it [the hunted game] so quickly, my son?"

Jacob, replied that, "The Lord your God gave me success."

Did you catch that?

Jacob said that God supernaturally assisted him in the killing of game.

Now, if God was/is so against hunting (as some idiots state) and Isaac was super-close (as the Scripture states he was) to this "anti-hunting God", don't you think Isaac would have called foul on Isaac's whopper that God supposedly helped him put the bam to Bambi? I do. However, the Lord's blessing on hunting and killing game passed the covenant father's BS Detector. It made Genesis 9:1-3 (i.e., biblical) sense to him; and the ruse worked because it was within reason to this godly man that a quick kill, via divine assistance, was well within the realm of the Scripture.

If it weren't, Isaac would have called him on it and shouted, "Sweet Jesus would never have helped you hunt a poor defenseless animal – you're the devil!" But, alas ... he didn't because God has not, nor ever will be, against the hunting and killing of game.

Boom! Put that in your anti-hunting pipe and smoke it.

Now, for those who have tried to pin Esau's wantonness somehow on hunting, allow me to correct you. Esau's sins had nothing to do with hunting. Esau's problem lay within the fact that he esteemed lightly his spiritual heritage; and according to the Scripture, he was pre-ordained to get bypassed.

It had zero to do with hunting because, as we have already established, God has blessed mankind with the righteous right to hunt. God's rejection of Esau predated his first hunting trip, duh. According to the apostle Paul, before Esau did anything his fate was sealed. Esau's rejection and Jacob's election had nada to do with anything either of them did (Rom.9:10-13). People who try to link Esau's missing out on the blessing with his penchant for hunting are missing the point of this ancient tale: it's all about God's choice, not man's will or his inherent goodness (Rom.9:14-18).

5 Leviticus 17:13

Leviticus 17:13

So when any man from the sons of Israel, or from the aliens who sojourn among them, in hunting catches a beast or a bird which may be eaten, he shall pour out its blood and cover it with earth. –Leviticus 17:13

The above hunting text, as denoted, was ripped out of the book of Leviticus. For those not in the biblical know, Leviticus is a book that Moses penned many, many moons ago to provide a holy glide path for the Israelites who had just been freed from being held captive by the idolatrous Egyptians for 400 years. The purpose of this charge was to peel away the Israelites from Egyptian influence and give them a distinct set of laws, pleasing to God, which would set 'em apart from polytheistic Egypt.

For instance, as you bounce through the book of Leviticus you'll note that there's a big emphasis on personal piety. God did not want them walking like an Egyptian. In addition, if and when an Israelite did screw up and sinned, this book is crystal clear regarding what must be done in order for them to have their muck-ups atoned for. The book of Leviticus meticulously addresses every aspect of the Israelites' life before Jehovah. Everything from how they're to worship, to what they're to eat, to what they're supposed to wear, to whom they're to have sex with and not have sex with; this exhaustive list of do's and don’ts covers it all … even hunting.

Now, granted, there’s not a heck of a lot about hunting, but what is and isn’t said about hunting sure says a lot to this hunter.

Let’s break the text down, shall we?

> So when any man from the sons of Israel, or from the aliens who sojourn among them, in hunting catches a beast or a bird which may be eaten, he shall pour out its blood and cover it with earth. –Leviticus 17:13

Please note that Moses didn’t say, “So when any man from the sons of Israel, or from the aliens who sojourn among them, in hunting catches a beast or a bird he should be looked at really weird by the twelve, non-hunting tribes of Israel and should thus be vociferously condemned as a murderer who killeth Winnie The Pooh.”

Did you notice it didn’t say that? Yeah, that’s not what old Moses said.

Moses also did not say, “Whosoever hunteth the beast which creeps upon the earth should be made to repent, muy pronto, before the sun sets, because, boy howdy, did he screw up!”

Also, please note that Moses did not say, “The damnable, evil hunter that killeth God’s sweet critters shouldest be stoned with many stones outside the camp.”

And lastly, nor did Moses say, “Woe unto him that shooteth the duck and/or the buck for in that act of shooting the duck and/or the buck doth the Lord God Almighty get really, really wroth with thee and becomes so sore displeased, to such an extent that he will infect thy rectum with a grievous and sore, festering butt itch for thy hunting!"

Nope. None of that stuff in this verse. The only thing the text calls for the hunter to do is, when he hunts and kills the animal he's going to eat the back straps thereof, he is to pour it's blood out upon the ground and cover it up with dust because blood is sacred to God and you ain't 'spose to eat or drink it. Duh.

That's it. No more. No less.

6
Thou Shall Not Kill
But Thou Shall Hunt

Giles
6/07

Thou Shall Not Kill, But Thou Shall Hunt

I wish I had a new gun for every time I've had an anti-hunter who (more often than not) is also an agnostic or an atheist, quote to me the sixth commandment, namely "Thou shall not kill" as a proof text against my God-blessed pursuit of hunting.

If I had a new gun, per misquote, from the desperate bunny lovers, then my battery would make Mark Muller's arsenal look like Ed Bagley, Jr's, because, OMG, do they toss that verse around like a drunken dwarf at a Kid Rock concert.

Now, before I examine the verse the anti-hunters fling about the most as an "ah-ha", gotcha proof text that "God's against hunting", let me ask my anti-hunting, pro-choice lovelies this question: how come you wizards don't play this card when talking about snuffing out the life of an unborn baby?

I hear you caterwaul about how wrong it is to make an omelet out of a whooping crane's eggs, but I don't hear you say squat about killing a helpless, defenseless baby in its mother's womb. You make the connection that an unborn whooping crane in an egg is a baby whooping crane but not so much with an unborn child in its mother's womb. What gives?

Oh, I'm sorry. I forgot. It's not yet a baby; it's a "fetus." Unless, of course, it's William and Kate's "Royal" baby, then it's a baby and not a fetus. Everyone else has fetuses, and when they call it a fetus versus a baby, then according to the progressives, you may, while it is in its mother's womb, crack its skull and suck its brain through a vacuum cleaner fitted with razor blades. My, how consistent you are with your interpretation and application of article Seis of the Decalogue. You go, girl!

Now, without further ado, herewith is my ham-fisted approach to the oft ill-quoted sixth comment in Moses' top ten list of do's and don'ts from Jehovah.

"Thou Shall Not Kill" - Exodus 20:13

If this commandment literally meant thou shall not kill anything, anywhere, at any time, for any reason, then God would be in deep weeds because, in the OT, he ordered animal sacrifices for sins; and in the OT and NT, just wars against evil enemies (Rom.13:1-3).

Also, if all killing is forbidden then Jesus could not be our savior because he facilitated the killing of fish by the hundreds (Jn.21:11) and ate the "murdered" meat. As Christians, we'd be screwed salvifically, if that were true, because atonement had to come from a sinless sacrifice. Right? Right.

"Thou shall not kill" does not mean kill per se, but thou shalt not murder. If you Google the sixth commandment like I did, Mr. and Mrs. Bunny Lover, you quickly see that a stack of Hebrew scholars from time immemorial translate the word "kill" as "thou not shall not murder" or kill unlawfully.

What the sixth commandment condemns is the intentional killing of another person. This passage is not talking about the uprooting and eating of a "murdered" carrot or the legal and ethical shooting of a deer, but the intentional snuffing out of a human life as in a premeditated murder, a sudden fit of rage, or in an unjust war, or abortion, euthanasia, infanticide, genocide and suicide.

> ... if all killing is forbidden then Jesus could not be our savior because he facilitated the killing of fish by the hundreds (Jn. 21:11) and ate the "murdered" meat. As Christians, we'd be screwed salvifically, if that were true, because atonement had to come from a sinless sacrifice. Right? Right.

For me, Genesis 9:1-6 sums up nicely what the sixth article of the Decalogue connotes:

Then God blessed Noah and his sons, saying to them, "Be fruitful and increase in number and fill the earth. The fear and dread of you will fall on all the beasts of the earth, and on all the birds in the sky, on every creature that moves along the ground, and on all the fish in the sea; they are given into your hands. Everything that lives and moves about will be food for you. Just as I gave you the green plants, I now give you everything. But you must not eat meat that has its lifeblood still in it. And for your lifeblood I will surely demand an accounting. I will demand an accounting from every animal. And from each human being, too, I will demand an accounting for the life of another human being. Whoever sheds human blood, by humans shall their blood be shed; for in the image of God has God made mankind.

God established that we could eat fruits, veggies, birds, fish and animals. The only way I know to get one of the aforementioned in the eating stage of the game is to, well, kill it. I guess you could wait until the carrot or critter died of old age but I'm a guessin' it wouldn't delight your palette too much, eh?

The forbidding of killing anything is in the murdering of another human being and not in the hunting a bobwhite quail.

7 God's Idea of Interior design

God's Idea of Interior Design

Have you ever watched Christian television? If so, have you ever paid particular attention to the décor of the various sound stages, or the churches that are highlighted via these networks?

To those who have watched Christian TV and have paid attention to their "style" did you notice the places were usually decked out with a lot of animal skins, sea-mammal hides and a bunch of awesome apex predators like eagles and lions or the formidable wild oxen of the world?

You didn't?

Yeah, me neither.

What one does see when he usually rocks up to Christian TV or at your nominal church in Light-A-Fart, Oregon? Well, it ain't taxidermy. It's not a profuse use of animal hides. It's not ferocious lions adorning the staircases, podiums or entrances. At least not normally.

No, in contrast to the aforementioned it is usually the following:

- Lavender or teal carpet.
- Pastel-colored flyers detailing all the weddings, baby showers, birthdays, picnics and covered dish dinners for that month.

- A Starbucks kiosk with trendy hipsters drinking a skinny latte in skinny jeans with a hairdo that puts the gel in evangelical.

- Floral arrangements that are so profuse that they make a FTD warehouse look like a dry gully outside of Slaton, Texas.

- As far as prints go, there's usually a lot of matching reproductions of fat baby angels in various Little Rascal poses that look like they have a good buzz going from mama's breast milk that's been liberally mixed with Mountain Dew and Percocet.

- Turning to the churches "fine" artwork, they commonly are depictions of Jesus, Peter and John the Baptist in aggravated states of angst, looking more like a soft-focused and melancholic Victorian woman who just found out she's got herpes rather than men who were masculine revolutionaries, heralds of truth, and rough pioneers of the greatest story ever told.

Bottom line, and by-n-large, in my enormously humble opinion, it's normally either a highly effeminized environment Christians have created or the place looks like the interior of a cheap comedy club down in Coconut Grove; or it's more Spartan than a college dorm room. Either way, none of the above strikes a good Hebrew sense of kabod to the congregant.

As you can tell, such an environment has zero appeal to me. Guess who else thinks it sucks? Um, that would be God. Yes, God and I have the same tastes when it comes to interior design, as we both like dead animals around and sculptures and fine art that remind us of nature's apex predators and animals.

God's Idea of Interior Design

How do I know what God would and would not like for a house of worship? Well, Dinky, it's spelled out rather clearly in this book called the Bible. Ever heard of it? In particularly, in the book of Exodus, chapter thirty-five.

Yep, Exodus 35 outlines the particulars God wanted his emancipated people to utilize in the tabernacle in which he would be glorified.

Check it out:

> Then Moses assembled all the congregation of the
> sons of Israel, and said to them, "These are the
> things that the LORD has commanded [you] to do:
>
> 2 "For six days work may be done, but on the
> seventh day you shall have a holy [day], a sabbath of
> complete rest to the LORD; whoever does any work on
> it shall be put to death. 3 You shall not kindle a fire in
> any of your dwellings on the sabbath day."
>
> 4 Moses spoke to all the congregation of the
> sons of Israel, saying, "This is the thing which the
> LORD has commanded, saying, 5 Take from among
> you a contribution to the LORD; whoever is
> of a willing heart, let him bring it as the
> LORD'S contribution: gold, silver, and bronze, 6
> and blue, purple and scarlet [material],
> fine linen, goats [hair], 7 and rams skins dyed red, and
> porpoise skins, and acacia wood, 8 and oil for
> lighting, and spices for the anointing oil, and
> for the fragrant incense, 9 and onyx stones and
> setting stones for the ephod and for the breastpiece.
>
> 10 Let every skillful man among you come, and

make all that the LORD has commanded: 11 the
tabernacle, its tent and its covering, its hooks and
its boards, its bars, its pillars, and its sockets; 12 the
ark and its poles, the mercy seat, and the curtain of
the screen; 13 the table and its poles, and all its
utensils, and the bread of the Presence; 14 the
lampstand also for the light and its utensils and its
lamps and the oil for the light; 15 and the altar of
incense and its poles, and the anointing oil and the
fragrant incense, and the screen for the doorway at
the entrance of the tabernacle; 16 the altar of
burnt offering with its bronze grating, its poles, and
all its utensils, the basin and its stand; 17 the
hangings of the court, its pillars and its sockets, and
the screen for the gate of the court; 18 the pegs of
the tabernacle and the pegs of the court and their
cords; 19the woven garments for ministering in the
holy place, the holy garments for Aaron the priest and
the garments of his sons, to minister as priests.'"

20 Then all the congregation of the sons of
Israel departed from Moses' presence.
21 Everyone whose heart stirred him and
everyone whose spirit moved him came [and]
brought the LORD'S contribution for the
work of the tent of meeting and for all its
service and for the holy garments. 22 Then
all whose hearts moved them, both men and
women, came [and] brought brooches and
earrings and signet rings and bracelets, all articles of
gold; so [did] every man who presented an

offering of gold to the LORD. 23 Every man, who had in his possession blue and purple and scarlet [material] and fine linen and goats' [hair] and rams' skins dyed red and porpoise skins, brought them. 24 Everyone who could make a contribution of silver and bronze brought the LORD'S contribution; and every man who had in his possession acacia wood for any work of the service brought it. 25 All the skilled women spun with their hands, and brought what they had spun, [in] blue and purple [and] scarlet [material] and [in] fine linen. 26 All the women whose heart stirred with a skill spun the goats' [hair]. 27 The rulers brought the onyx stones and the stones for setting for the ephod and for the breastpiece; 28 and the spice and the oil for the light and for the anointing oil and for the fragrant incense. 29 The Israelites, all the men and women, whose heart moved them to bring [material] for all the work, which the LORD had commanded through Moses to be done, brought a freewill offering to the LORD.

30 Then Moses said to the sons of Israel, "See, the LORD has called by name Bezalel the son of Uri, the son of Hur, of the tribe of Judah. 31 "And He has filled him with the Spirit of God, in wisdom, in understanding and in knowledge and in all craftsmanship; 32 to make designs for working in gold and in silver and in bronze, 33 and in the cutting of stones for settings and in the carving of wood, so as to perform in every inventive work. 34 "He also has put in

> his heart to teach, both he and Oholiab, the son of
> Ahisamach, of the tribe of Dan. 35 “He has filled them
> with skill to perform every work of an engraver and
> of a designer and of an embroiderer, in blue and in
> purple [and] in scarlet [material], and in fine linen, and
> of a weaver, as performers of every work and
> makers of designs.

Okay, class. Lets go back through that detailed list of design goodies that God wanted dressing out his house of praise and unpack its contents slowly and see what the Lord God employed. Cool? Cool.

So, what do we have?

Let’s see … we’ve got gold, silver, and bronze.

We also have blue, purple and scarlet material.

In addition, we have acacia wood, oil for lighting, spices for the anointing oil, fragrant incense, onyx stones and setting stones, together with lampstands, utensils, poles, woven garments, fine linen and … and … shoot, what am I missing?

Let’s see: Incense? Check. Gold? Check. Red drapes? Check. Anointing oil? Check.

Man, I feel like I’m forgetting something. What did I miss? I’m so stupid.

Oh, now I remember.

I forgot that God special ordered goat hair, ram skins and … wait for it … wait … wait … (could I get a drum roll please?) … Here it comes … porpoise skins!

God's Idea of Interior Design

Wow. Talk about being politically incorrect. God ordered a stack of Flipper pelts to adorn his tent of meeting. Porpoise skins? Yep, porpoise skins.

I've got to admit that when I read porpoise skins, as politically incorrect as I am, I, your humble correspondent, even balked at that one. Being uncertain that what I read was legit I did what any half- decent sleuth does and started digging around in various translations and headed for the original Hebrew word. Before I dissect the Hebrew word, here's how several other translators spin the word "porpoise" in Exodus 35:7:

King James Version:

> And rams' skins dyed red, and badgers' skins, and shittim wood,

New American Standard:

> and rams' skins dyed red, and porpoise skins, and acacia wood,

New International Version:

> ram skins dyed red and hides of sea cows; acacia wood;

American Standard Version:

> and rams' skins dyed red, and sealskins, and acacia wood,

Douay-Rheims:

> And rams' skins dyed red, and violet coloured skins, setim wood,

English Standard Version:

> tanned rams' skins, and goatskins; acacia wood,

Hebrew Names Version:

> rams' skins dyed red, sea cow hides, shittim wood,

Holman Christian Standard Bible:

ram skins dyed red and manatee skins; acacia wood;

New International Reader's Version:

ram skins that are dyed red the hides of sea cows
acacia wood

New King James Version:

ram skins dyed red, badger skins, and acacia wood;

The Darby Translation:

and rams' skins dyed red, and badgers' skins, and
acacia-wood,

The Message:

tanned rams' skins; dolphin skins; acacia wood;

I don't know about you guys but plowing through that list didn't help very much either. Matter of fact, I feel like a termite in a yo-yo, I'm so confused.

Did you catch the various critters the translators tossed up?

- badger
- sea cows
- seals
- manatees
- dolphins
- porpoises

Uh, earth to Bible translators: there's a big difference between a badger and a sea cow. Hello!

That's like saying it could either be a wolverine or a hammer-head shark. Or, akin to describing the girl you met at church and asked out to dinner, saying that she kinda looks like either Jennifer Aniston or Roseanne Barr. How many of you know there's a big, BIG, difference between those two chicas?

Wow. Talk about being politically incorrect. God ordered a stack of Flipper pelts to adorn his tent of meeting. Porpoise skins? Yep, porpoise skins.

In all fairness to the majority of the aforementioned translations, they are all pretty close in their consensus that whatever that bugger was, it dug the water. But a badger? Really? A badger?

Unconvinced and unready to go to print with *The New American Standard's* take on Exodus 35:7, I soldiered on into the Hebrew. What was/is the original Hebrew word used in this ancient text?

Full disclaimer: I know as much about Hebrew as I do a woman's innermost needs, so I went to a Hebrew scholar I know via Facebook and he directed me to this resource for the skinny on the badger-porpoise conundrum.

According to the Bible-History.com, the word used for "porpoise" skins is the Hebrew word – *tachash*. Check it out ...

> The word *tachash* occurs in the descriptions of the tabernacle in Ex. 25; 26; 35; 36 and 39, in the directions for moving the tabernacle as given in Nu. 4, and in only one other passage, Ezek. 16:10, where Jerusalem is spoken of as a maiden clothed and adorned by her Lord.
>
> In nearly all these passages the word *tachash* occurs with `or, "skin," rendered: the King James Version

"badgers' skins," the Revised Version (British and American) "sealskin," the Revised Version, margin "porpoise-skin."

In all the passages cited in Exodus and Numbers these skins are mentioned as being used for coverings of the tabernacle; in Ezek 16:10, for shoes or sandals. The Septuagint rendering would mean purple or blue skins, which however is not favored by Talmudic writers or by modern grammarians, who incline to believe that *tachash* is the name of an animal.

The rendering, "badger," is favored by the Talmudic writers and by the possible etymological connection of the word with the Latin taxus and the German Dachs. The main objection seems to be that badgers' skins would probably not have been easily available to the Israelites. The badger, *Meles taxus*, while fairly abundant in Lebanon and Anti-Lebanon, does not seem to occur in Sinai or Egypt.

A seal, *Monachus albiventer* (Arabic fukmeh), the porpoise, *Phocoena comrnunis*, and the common dolphin, *Delphinus delphis*, are all found in the Mediterranean.

The dugong (sea cow 5 to 9ft. in length), Halicore dugong, inhabits the Indian Ocean and adjoining waters from the Red Sea to Australia. The Arabic *tukhas* or *dukhas* is near to *tachash* and is applied to the dolphin, which is also called delfin. It may be used also for the porpoise or even the seal, and is said by Tristram and others to be applied to the dugong...

> The dugong of the Indian Ocean and the manatee of the Atlantic and of certain rivers of Africa and South America, are the only living representatives of the Sirenia. A third species, the sea-cow of Behring Sea, became extinct in the 18th century. The seal and porpoise of the Revised Version (British and American), the dolphin, and the dugong are all of about the same size and all inhabit the seas bordering on Egypt and Sinai, so that all are possible candidates for identification with the tachash. Of the four, recent opinion seems most to favor the dugong.[1]

Yikes. Intense, eh? Who'd a thunk there'd be that much concern and sweat over what type of animal lost its skin for Jehovah's holy digs? Anyway, it looks like the scholars boiled it down to a dugong or a sea-cow.

Please, no one tell Hayden Panettiere. She'd be inconsolable and probably never come to church again.

Here's my walk-away from that tortured Bible study: it looks as if it was a big sea mammal versus a badger. However, one thing that is undeniable is that regardless of what animal it was, it was not a domestic critter and therefore, it had to be hunted.

No doubt someone will say, "well that was way back in the caveman days when people were swinging off trees like monkeys and there wasn't a Home Depot or a Bed, Bath and Beyond to purchase more sophisticated adornments for Jehovah's church in the wilderness."

Uh, I don't know if you missed it or not, but it clearly states the

---

1. http://www.bib-history.com/isbe/B/BADGER/

Here's my walk-away from that tortured Bible study: it looks as if it was a big sea mammal versus a badger. However, one thing that is undeniable is that regardless of what animal it was, it was not a domestic critter and therefore, it had to be hunted.

people of God had all the fancy and funky materials of various colors with all kinds of precious metals to boot. And … and … with all these accouterments God still special ordered animal rugs. He could have easily had a lovely place for his boys and girls to worship in minus the dead beasts, but guess what? He didn't.

What I also find interesting, amusing and in contrast with today's sassy believers is that the people of God actually had goat, ram and porpoise skins to donate to God's building program. I'd bet you can't show me too many God followers nowadays who would have a surplus of animal skins should they be called upon to donate them for the church's new sanctuary.

Standards

Another interesting little ditty found in the Old Testament was the various standards or flags that represented the twelve tribes of Israel. In our vernacular it would be akin to the footballs teams mascot. Of note, and keeping with the hunting/wild game theme of the twelve standards, we've got three predators, one bad-ass bull, a stubborn animal who'll bite the crap out of you, and a beautiful stag.

> **LION:** ***Judah:*** Judah, you, your brothers shall acknowledge; your hand will be at your enemies'

nape; your father's sons will prostrate themselves to you. A lion cub is Judah; from the prey, my son, you elevated yourself. He crouches, lies down like a lion, and like an awesome lion, who dares rouse him? The scepter shall not depart from Judah nor a scholar from among his descendants until Shiloh arrives and his will be an assemblage of nations. He will tie his donkey to the vine; to the vine branch his donkey's foal; he will launder his garments in wine and his robe in the blood of grapes. Red eyed from wine, and white toothed from milk.

Judah's banner reflects the above verse spoken prophetically right before the death of his father Jacob. (See Genesis 49:8 - 12.)

DONKEY: ***Issachar:*** Issachar, is a strong-boned donkey; he rests between the boundaries. He saw tranquility that it was good, and the land that it was pleasant, yet he bent his shoulder to bear and he became an indentured laborer. (See Genesis 49:14 – 15.)

WILD BULL: ***Ephraim:*** But Israel extended his right hand and laid it on Ephraim's head though he was the younger and his left hand on Manasseh's head. He maneuvered his hands , for Manasseh was the firstborn. He blessed Joseph and he said, O God before Whom my forefathers Abraham and Isaac walked -- God Who shepherds me from my inception until this day: May the angel who redeems me from all evil bless the lads, and may my name be declared upon them, and the names of my forefathers Abraham and Isaac, and may they proliferate abundantly like fish within the land. … So he blessed them that day, saying, "By you shall Israel bless saying, 'May God make you like Ephraim and like Manasseh'" -- and he put Ephraim before Manasseh. (See Genesis 48:13 – 20.)

WOLF: *Benjamin:* Benjamin, is a predatory wolf; in the morning he will devour prey and in the evening he will distribute spoils. (See Genesis 49:27.)

SERPENT: *Dan:* Dan, will avenge his people, the tribes of Israel will be united as one. Dan will be a serpent on the highway, a viper by the path, that bites a horse's heels so its rider falls backward. For Your salvation do I long, O Hashem! (See Genesis 49:16 – 18.)

HIND [RED OR FALLOW DEER]:
Naphtali: Naphtali, is a hind let loose who delivers beautiful sayings. (See Genesis 49:20.)

God's people aligned themselves from a decorative standpoint with the ultimate hunters in the animal kingdom: the lion, the wolf, serpent. Or a powerful wild bull or the ultimate, gorgeous game animal, the red stag. Why do I think they choose these beasts? Well they were awesome and through interacting with them in the hunt they obviously sported enviable characteristics that God wanted them to emulate.

God's Idea of Interior Design

Solomon's Crib

1 Kings 10:19

> There were six steps to the throne and a round top to the throne at its rear, and arms on each side of the seat, and two lions standing beside the arms.

1 Kings 10:20

> Twelve lions were standing there on the six steps on the one side and on the other; nothing like it was made for any other kingdom.

PLEASE NOTE:
Also, later on when the people of God had at their disposal the Psalms, they actually sang songs, worshiped God and said prayers that were laced with hunting analogies. Man, how we have fallen away from that spirit- inspired liturgical perch, eh? The songs we sing are syrupy little love songs that sound like something Selena Gomez would write about her high school crush.

Finally, I'm fully aware that the scripture clearly shows that God doesn't dwell in temples made by human hands and that there's not a special building in which he hangs out and the church is indeed the gathering of the elect and not a prefab metal building. However, I do find it interesting that the places where Jesus preached a lot of sermons were in the great outdoors. He did a lot of his teaching and miracles around fishing and fishermen, which entails the capturing, killing and eating of God's creation. Ah, learning about God in the great outdoors. I think in our puerile environments we miss a lot not being out in the elements and all the wildness and lessons they afford us. In the Old Testament God brought the outside in and in the New Testament Jesus brought indoor boys outside for his heavenly lessons around the fishing connection.

> *We shape our buildings, and afterwards our buildings shape us.* – Winston Churchill

8 The Prophets and Poets Profuse Use of Hunting Parallels

AFRICA'S BLACK
DEATH
giles
12/08

The Prophets and Poets Profuse Use of Hunting Parallels

As stated, there isn't a heck of a lot of direct references about the people of God hunting. For that matter there's not a whole lot of references to them taking a crap either.

Matter of fact, there's hardly any passages about them: breathing,

or walking,
or waving hello or good-bye,
or picking their noses,
or farting,
or shooting Shlomo the bird when he did something stupid,
or scratching their Chattahoochee canal when it got itchy during a hot summer sweat,
or playing with their dogs,
or having sex,
or gambling on camel races,
or writing their name in the snow when they peed,
or making fun of Elisha's bald spot

But you and I both know they probably did the above-mentioned with great regularity with the exception of writing their name in the snow when they peed because it doesn't snow that much in Israel.

So, what's my point?

Well, my argument is that, just because there's not a stack of chapters or a Reality Show given to the exploits of the various Israelites' hunting endeavors, it doesn't mean that they didn't do it.

As argued in the previous chapters, it is clear that they did exercise their God-ordained right to hunt because:

a). We've already examined several scriptures that stated that hunting was God's idea to begin with and ...

b). Their tables were loaded with wild game. And you can bet your last shekel that a gazelle didn't willingly jump on Jehoshaphat's plate.

One thing that leads me to believe hunting was more pervasive than the anti-hunting lovelies would lead you to believe is that the language of the biblical poets and prophets, inspired by the Holy Spirit (2Tim.3:16), is laced with hunting analogies. I'm talkin', it is profusely strewn throughout their communiqués from God to his people.

Now, you have to help me here because, remember, I ain't the coldest beer in the fridge, but don't you think an all-knowing and all-wise, loving God both wants and knows best how to communicate his message to the people he's trying to reach?

What do I mean?

Well, think about it in our context. Say God spawned some new directives for people in America, (which he wouldn't), and our eternal souls hinged upon our understanding and obeying them, and he utilized analogies drawn from the game of the English sport of cricket.

If he did that, I think it would be (forgive me, Lord) both ignorant and/or calloused at best, as most Americans would not know what in the heck God was talking about. Those idioms and analogies would be completely out of the ballpark for the average American baseball enthusiast who doesn't know nor give a flibbertigibbet about cricket. Cricket? Please.

Yep, we would be lost in space because we would have no clue what the Holy One was talking about. Like I said, it would be a combo of bad communication skills motivated by either ignorance or evil and we know God's not either.

No, when God cues up to get his message across, the consummate communicator is going to use expressions and parallels that would be immediately understood by the people he's trying to reach. He's going to speak to their context, what was commonplace to them, because if he didn't his people aren't going to understand squat, they're going to end up displeasing God and roasting for all eternity in hell; and God wouldn't want that, eh?

Therefore, the Lord, when he chose to converse, used analogies, types, shadows, similes, etc. that are going to speak to what they know, you know, stuff that relates to their lives like farming, ranching, commerce, familial relationships and wait for it … hunting.

Indeed, my little darlings, the hunting analogies are profuse. Therefore, this author must conclude that the people of God were so steeped in a hunting culture that when the prophets and poets utilized these figures of speech they got the message that God wanted them to receive.

What follows is just a sliver of the hunting portraits God utilized to paint divine truth. Even though it's just a sliver and not an exhaustive list, it is overwhelming. The following verses are taken only from Job, the Psalms, Proverbs, Ecclesiastes and the Prophets. Enjoy.

Surely he shall deliver thee from the snare of the fowler, and from the noisome pestilence. – Ps. 91:3 (KJV)

When David cued up to describe how God delivers the believer from their enemies, namely the lust of the flesh, the lust of the eyes and the boastful pride of life, he didn't use a knitting analogy, or whiffle ball analogy or a badminton analogy. He drafted a simile from the realm of hunting.

"Surely he shall deliver thee from the snare of the fowler ..."

Most indoor boys today don't know what the heck a "fowler" is. But David did. And the people of God did. And the Holy Spirit, who, according the word of God inspired this text, did; and he spurred David to craft this word picture because, I'm assuming, the people of God would immediately comprehend what salvation would look like in real time to the redeemed. It would be like a bird escaping from a hunter's trap, and these hunters understood what God would be to them because they hunted. Hello!

A fowler, for those not in the know, is a hunter who hunts birds with traps and or snares, i.e. -- hidden devices or nooses that choke to death unsuspecting birds. Yep, to be certain, it was a brutal way to die, and the inspired psalmist said that it is those who "dwell in the shelter of the Most High and abide in the shadow of the Almighty" who get free from the "fowler's" deadly "snares."

Indeed, my little darlings, the hunting analogies are profuse. Therefore, this author must conclude that the people of God were so steeped in a hunting culture that when the prophets and poets utilized these figures of speech they got the message that God wanted them to receive.

Mostly, Christian softies today wouldn't use a hunting analogy to describe how God protects the believer, but God, via David, did and that's why I'd rather go to David's church than theirs.

The snare analogy, utilized by poets and the prophets, is profuse. I'm talkin' it's overkill, pardon the pun – which pushes me to conclude everyone was muy familiar with this form of capture, kill and eat.

Here's a couple of more examples.

Deliver thyself as a roe from the hand of the hunter, and as a bird from the hand of the fowler. – Prov.6:5

Our soul is escaped as a bird out of the snare of the fowlers: the snare is broken, and we are escaped. – Ps.124:7

And here, for further proof and for your viewing enjoyment, is a nice little list of other places the biblical authors used the word "snare."

Snare (New American Standard)

Exodus 10:7
Pharaoh's servants said to him, "How long will this man be a snare to us? Let the men go, that they may serve the Lord their God. Do you not realize that Egypt is destroyed?"

Exodus 23:33
They shall not live in your land, because they will make you sin against Me; for if you serve their gods, it will surely be a snare to you."

Exodus 34:12
Watch yourself that you make no covenant with the inhabitants of the land into which you are going, or it will become a snare in your midst.

Deuteronomy 7:16
You shall consume all the peoples whom the Lord your God will deliver to you; your eye shall not pity them, nor shall you serve their gods, for that would be a snare to you.

Deuteronomy 7:25
The graven images of their gods you are to burn with fire; you shall not covet the silver or the gold that is on them, nor take it for yourselves, or you will be snared by it, for it is an abomination to the Lord your God.

Joshua 23:13
know with certainty that the Lord your God will not continue to drive these nations out from before you; but they will be a snare and a trap to you, and a whip on your sides and thorns in your eyes, until you perish from off this good land which the

Lord your God has given you.

1 Samuel 18:21
Saul thought, "I will give her to him that she may become a snare to him, and that the hand of the Philistines may be against him." Therefore Saul said to David, "For a second time you may be my son-in-law today."

1 Samuel 28:9
But the woman said to him, "Behold, you know what Saul has done, how he has cut off those who are mediums and spiritists from the land. Why are you then laying a snare for my life to bring about my death?"

2 Samuel 22:6
The cords of Sheol surrounded me; The snares of death confronted me.

Job 18:9
"A snare seizes him by the heel, And a trap snaps shut on him.

Job 22:10
"Therefore snares surround you, And sudden dread terrifies you,

Job 34:30
So that godless men would not rule Nor be snares of the people.

Psalm 9:16
The Lord has made Himself known; He has executed judgment. In the work of his own hands the wicked is snared. Higgaion Selah.

Psalm 11:6

Upon the wicked He will rain snares; Fire and brimstone and burning wind will be the portion of their cup.

Psalm 18:5

The cords of Sheol surrounded me; The snares of death confronted me.

Psalm 38:12

Those who seek my life lay snares for me; And those who seek to injure me have threatened destruction, And they devise treachery all day long.

Psalm 64:5

They hold fast to themselves an evil purpose; They talk of laying snares secretly; They say, "Who can see them?"

Psalm 69:22

May their table before them become a snare; And when they are in peace, may it become a trap.

Psalm 91:3

For it is He who delivers you from the snare of the trapper And from the deadly pestilence.

Psalm 106:36

And served their idols, Which became a snare to them.

Psalm 119:110

The wicked have laid a snare for me, Yet I have not gone astray from Your precepts.

Psalm 124:7

Our soul has escaped as a bird out of the snare of the trapper; The snare is broken and we have escaped.

The Prophets and the Poets Profuse Use of Hunting Parallels

Psalm 140:5

The proud have hidden a trap for me, and cords; They have spread a net by the wayside; They have set snares for me. Selah.

Psalm 141:9

Keep me from the jaws of the trap which they have set for me, And from the snares of those who do iniquity.

Proverbs 6:2

If you have been snared with the words of your mouth, Have been caught with the words of your mouth,

Proverbs 7:23

Until an arrow pierces through his liver; As a bird hastens to the snare, So he does not know that it will cost him his life.

Proverbs 13:14

The teaching of the wise is a fountain of life, To turn aside from the snares of death.

Proverbs 14:27

The fear of the Lord is a fountain of life, That one may avoid the snares of death.

Proverbs 18:7

A fool's mouth is his ruin, And his lips are the snare of his soul.

Proverbs 22:5

Thorns and snares are in the way of the perverse; He who guards himself will be far from them.

Proverbs 22:25

Or you will learn his ways And find a snare for yourself.

Proverbs 29:25
The fear of man brings a snare, But he who trusts in the Lord will be exalted.

Ecclesiastes 7:26
And I discovered more bitter than death the woman whose heart is snares and nets, whose hands are chains. One who is pleasing to God will escape from her, but the sinner will be captured by her.

Ecclesiastes 9:12
Moreover, man does not know his time: like fish caught in a treacherous net and birds trapped in a snare, so the sons of men are ensnared at an evil time when it suddenly falls on them.

Isaiah 8:14

"Then He shall become a sanctuary; But to both the houses of Israel, a stone to strike and a rock to stumble over, And a snare and a trap for the inhabitants of Jerusalem.

Isaiah 8:15
"Many will stumble over them, Then they will fall and be broken; They will even be snared and caught."

Isaiah 24:17
Terror and pit and snare Confront you, O inhabitant of the earth.

Isaiah 24:18
Then it will be that he who flees the report of disaster will fall into the pit, And he who climbs out of the pit will be caught in the snare; For the windows above are opened, and the foundations of the earth shake.

The Prophets and the Poets Profuse Use of Hunting Parallels

Isaiah 28:13

So the word of the Lord to them will be, "Order on order, order on order, Line on line, line on line, A little here, a little there," That they may go and stumble backward, be broken, snared and taken captive.

Jeremiah 18:22

May an outcry be heard from their houses, When You suddenly bring raiders upon them; For they have dug a pit to capture me And hidden snares for my feet.

Jeremiah 48:43

"Terror, pit and snare are coming upon you, O inhabitant of Moab," declares the Lord.

Jeremiah 48:44

"The one who flees from the terror Will fall into the pit, And the one who climbs up out of the pit Will be caught in the snare; For I shall bring upon her, even upon Moab, The year of their punishment," declares the Lord.

Jeremiah 50:24

"I set a snare for you and you were also caught, O Babylon, While you yourself were not aware; You have been found and also seized Because you have engaged in conflict with the Lord."

Ezekiel 12:13

I will also spread My net over him, and he will be caught in My snare. And I will bring him to Babylon in the land of the Chaldeans; yet he will not see it, though he will die there.

Ezekiel 17:20

I will spread My net over him, and he will be caught in My snare. Then I will bring him to Babylon and enter into judgment with him there regarding the unfaithful act which he has committed against Me.

Hosea 5:1

[The People's Apostasy Rebuked] Hear this, O priests! Give heed, O house of Israel! Listen, O house of the king! For the judgment applies to you, For you have been a snare at Mizpah And a net spread out on Tabor.

Hosea 9:8

Ephraim was a watchman with my God, a prophet; Yet the snare of a bird catcher is in all his ways, And there is only hostility in the house of his God.

Romans 11:9

And David says, "Let their table become a snare and a trap, And a stumbling block and a retribution to them.

1 Timothy 3:7

And he must have a good reputation with those outside the church, so that he will not fall into reproach and the snare of the devil.

1 Timothy 6:9

But those who want to get rich fall into temptation and a snare and many foolish and harmful desires which plunge men into ruin and destruction.

The Prophets and the Poets Profuse Use of Hunting Parallels

2 *Timothy* 2:26

and they may come to their senses and escape from
the snare of the devil, having been held captive by him to do his will.

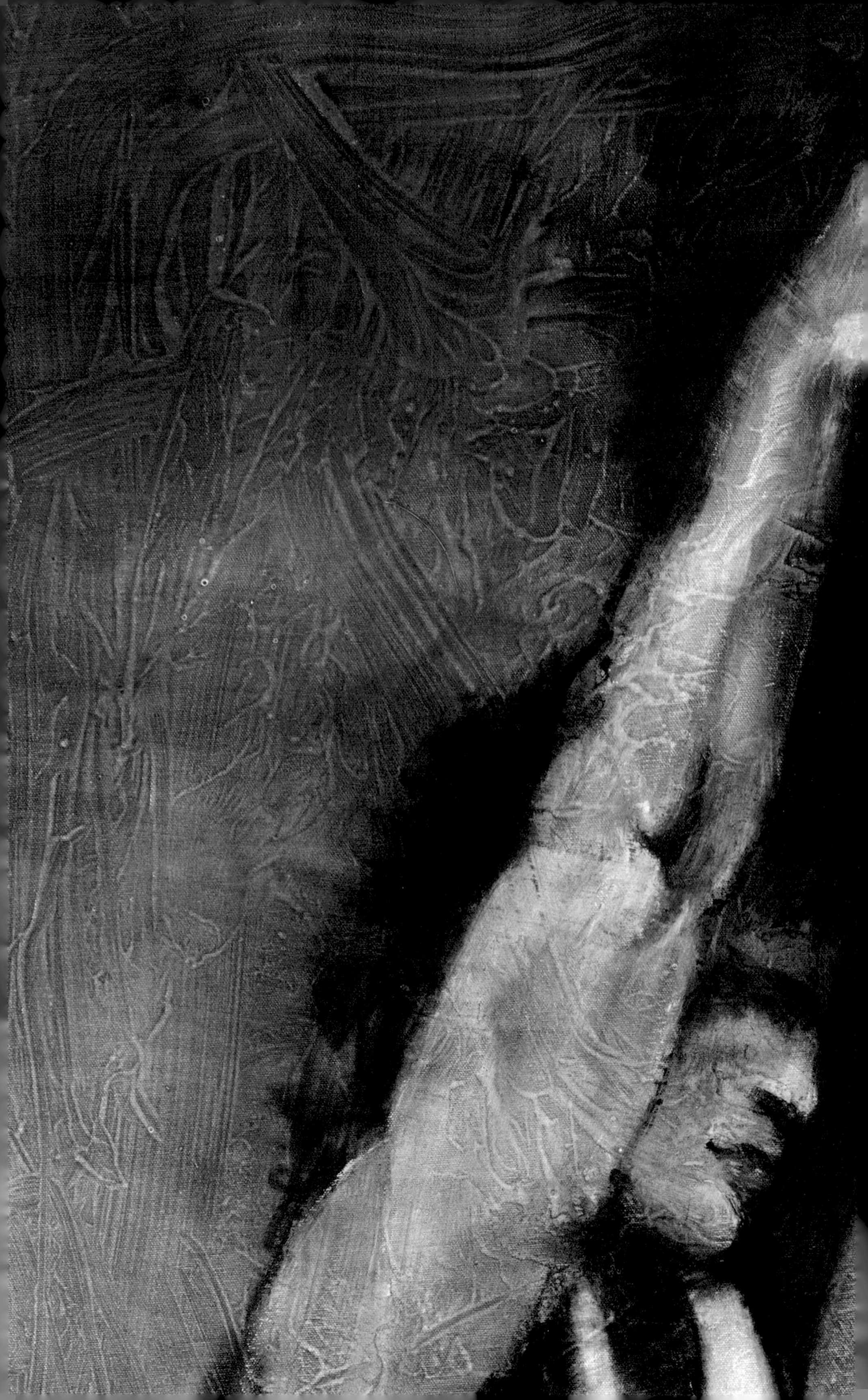

9 David's Confidence That He Could Kill Goliath Came from Killing Apex Predators

David's Confidence That He Could Kill Goliath Came from Killing Apex Predators

25 The men of Israel said, «Have you seen this man who
is coming up? Surely he is coming up to defy Israel. And
it will be that the king will enrich the man who kills him
with great riches and will give him his daughter and
make his father's house free in Israel.»

26 Then David spoke to the men who were
standing by him, saying, "What will be
done for the man who kills this Philistine and
takes away the reproach from Israel? For who is
this uncircumcised Philistine, that he should taunt the
armies of the living God?" 27 The people answered him
in accord with this word, saying, "Thus it will be
done for the man who kills him."

28 Now Eliab his oldest brother heard when he
spoke to the men; and Eliab's anger burned against
David and he said, "Why have you come down? And
with whom have you left those few sheep in
the wilderness? I know your insolence and the
wickedness of your heart; for you have come down in
order to see the battle." 29 But David said, "What have
I done now? Was it not just a question?" 30
Then he turned away from him to another and
said the same thing; and the people answered the

same thing as before.

31 When the words which David spoke were
heard, they told [them] to Saul, and he sent for
him. 32 David said to Saul, "Let no man's heart fail on
account of him; your servant will go and fight with
this Philistine." 33 Then Saul said to David, "You are
not able to go against this Philistine to fight with
him; for you are [but] a youth while he has been a
warrior from his youth." 34 But David said to Saul,
"Your servant was tending his father's sheep. When
a lion or a bear came and took a lamb from the
flock, 35 I went out after him and attacked him, and
rescued [it] from his mouth; and when he rose up
against me, I seized [him] by his beard and struck him
and killed him. 36 Your servant has killed both the
lion and the bear; and this uncircumcised Philistine will
be like one of them, since he has taunted the
armies of the living God." 37 And David said, "The
LORD who delivered me from the paw of the lion and
from the paw of the bear, He will deliver me from
the hand of this Philistine." And Saul said to David,
"Go, and may the LORD be with you."

Pretty much everyone and his dog are familiar with David's epic downing of the Philistines' champion, Goliath. Movies have been made about this ruddy teenager taking his simple slingshot against this blathering monster and dropping him like a bad habit.

Not only did David down the blasphemous jackass, he also took Goliath's own sword and decapitated him. Y'know, just to make certain that he doesn't pop back up like Jason Voorhees and terrify any further Israel's feckless "forces."

The narrative of David smoking Gath's greatest is the stuff of legends; an inspiring tale of faith and determination against staggering odds and, truth be told, against the disdain and unbelief of his jealous and beleaguered brethren.

I dig this story so much I did an oil painting from Gustave Dore's famous lithograph to adorn my walls, so that when I wake up in the morning and see little David holding Goliath's severed, blood-dripping noggin it can inspire me to not be a wuss, but rather have faith and go face the "giants" in my life. Life imitates art. And, as far as I'm concerned, it beats the crap out of a "Just Hang in There" cat poster.

As familiar as this story is, what I've seldom heard pontificated upon was that David got his godly confidence to kill this foul Philistine via the prior slaying of a lion and a bear.

Did you catch that little ditty in the aforementioned text?

I did.

Check it out: God's people, initially, tried to discourage David from taking Goliath on. They wanted him to be a scared punk like they were and just sit on the sidelines of life and complain about the problem instead of destroying the beast by facing it head on.

Thankfully, David was not persuaded by their pathetic, pusillanimous, faith-eviscerating words. Yep, the young shepherd was having none of his puny bros fear and unbelief; and the thing that put him over the top with holy confidence was not an Amy Grant song but the fact that God (his words, not mine: v.34, 37) enabled him to kill a lion and a bear; and the same God that empowered him to dispatch two apex predators was going to help him fell this mouthy maggot who's talking smack about God and his people.

Now, help me here: if killing animals is a sin, then why did the Lord God deliver David from certain death by supernaturally assisting this young lad to slay these four-legged marauders? Aw, did that ruin your "God hates killing animals" fairy tale?

Oh, and by the way, it was not recorded whether or not David ate these two would be sheep stealers after he whacked them — which highlights the fact that not every animal killed in the Scripture became table fare.

I just thought I'd point that out for you. You're welcome.

Lastly, I hope when I get to heaven I get to watch the video of David (with the psalmist and the millions of other hunters who're adorning heaven's bleachers) killing the lion, the bear and Goliath. That would be a great evening, eh? I'll bring the cigars and the popcorn. Jesus will supply the wine.

10 Jesus Christ: Lord, Savior, Fish Slayer and Meat Eater

10 Jesus Christ: Lord, Savior, Fish-Slayer and Meat Eater

Being a vegetarian nowadays is so trendy.

It's so, chic.

Those who only eat murdered veggies will tell you with chest swelling pride that they are vegetarians, even if you don't give a crap what they eat or don't eat.

They'll tell you anyway. Oh, yes they will.

And when they do tell you, they'll always do it with that Gwyneth Paltrow glare of disdain that flows from a sense of culinary preeminence over you, you meat-eating troglodyte.

Yep, the reason they feel the need to bray to the world that they prefer beets to beef is that they feel that eating rabbit food somehow makes them superior to your meat-munching, moron.

Y'know, when it comes to moral superiority I think the vacuous vegetarians, especially the ubiquitous starlets in Hollywood, should shut their meatless quiche holes.

Look, brain-soft, baby spinach people: not eating meat doesn't make you holy. It just makes you protein deficient; and eventually sick. But holy? Eh, not so much.

Oh, and as long as you're lecturing us meat eaters about the

Y'know, when it comes to moral superiority I think the vacuous vegetarians, especially the ubiquitous starlets in Hollywood, should shut their meatless quiche holes.

"evils" of consuming "murdered meat" you might want to tame that refrain if you own any of the following: a leather purse, leather shoes, leather belt, leather luggage, leather couch, leather chair, leather car seats, leather steering wheel, leather pants, leather mini skirt, leather bustier or anything else made of leather because they, too, equate the death of an animal. I'm sure you want to be seen as consistent and not viewed as a daft, duplicitous hypocrite, right?

D'oh. I almost forgot.

Here's another FYI for the vegetarians. For you to have your precious vegetables a farmer had to kill rabbits, deer, wild boar, birds and other animals that prey on your special grub.

It's true. Ask a farmer. I dare you.

I know a farmer down here in south Florida who has armed guards protecting his produce around the clock, trying to keep wild boar and deer from destroying your yummy greens. They kill hundreds of crop raiding pigs every year and it still doesn't deter them. The only thing that they have found that works to ward off said swine is to line their fields with AM transistor radios that blare Mexican music 24/7.

It's real. It's science.

The only way to be certain no animal was harmed in your food selection is to take special care to buy your produce and eat at restaurants that only sell and serve veggies harvested from special boutique gardens that are guaranteed, "No Animals Got Harmed" farms. That's what Frank Miniter told me to tell you.

Oh, and riddle me this: if you love animals so much why do you eat their food? That's so wrong. Especially with global warming and diminishing resources just around the corner. What will they eat, you evil, animal-food eater, if you are competing with them in consuming these limited and thinning resources?

Now, in regards to what one eats or doesn't eat, I truly don't give a flibbertigibbet. I've got no beef with silent vegetarians who, for whatever reason, choose not to eat meat. However, it is the holier-than-thous that tick me off when they come off as ethically excellent because they grub vegetables versus venison.

When I moved from my meat eating, west Texas roots to the tres chic city of Miami, I met a cluster of vegetarians. What I found interesting, as they looked aghast at my "unethical" entrée selection, is that these meat-bemoaners usually led very unethical lives.

Here's another FYI for the vegetarians. For you to have your precious vegetables a farmer had to kill rabbits, deer, wild boar, birds and other animals that prey on your special grub.

As I type this, I'm thinking about those who gave me the most grief over hunting and eating meat; and of this rogues' gallery, I remember clearly several of them were whores (not professionally, but socially), pro-abortion, had kids out of wedlock, cheated on taxes, were unethical in business, were constant liars, scammers, drunks, lazy bellies, evil beasts and adulterers -- and those were just the Christians.

But, by golly, they didn't eat meat.

Hey, immoral vegans: do you think vegetarianism offsets your sins? Is lettuce now to be equated with a medieval indulgence? Will the eating of edamame beans offset your *ménage à trois* with the bartender and busboy from Chili's last night, and thereby expedite your release from purgatory sooner than expected? Is this your hope?

If one wants to look to someone superior and follow him or her as to what or what not to grub, then I think we should not look to anyone currently schlepping the third rock from the sun. I know for me and my casa, instead of eyeing a Hollywood harlot's food choice, we're going to look to the Holiest of All and what he dined on for our life's culinary glide path. Call us crazy.

Which brings me to this enquiry: What did Jesus grub on when he donned an earth suit 2000 years ago? Boy, that sure would be interesting to find out, eh?

When it comes to talking about someone being superior in the purest/ultimate sense of the word, well ... Jesus leaves us all in the dust, right? I mean, how can we compete with someone who's perfect? Seeing that he never sinned in word or in deed, which includes what he ate and drank, I wonder what he banqueted on when he sat down at Denny's way back in the day?

Did he order:

- Barbecued aubergine on lentil polenta patties with a black bean sauce?

- Or was it a Best in Class Tomato Tart?
- I know, it was Chinese tea eggs with a noodle salad. Dee-Lish!
- No, wait. It had to be the sassy and crunchy Red Lentil Kofte.
- Or possibly a baked globe artichoke with a Parmesan soufflé.
- Lord forgive me for forgetting that it could've been a boutique falafel cupcake.
- Or, the rape oil crackers with orange, fennel and feta salad.
- What is wrong with me? More than likely, it was a garbanzo bean pita, lightly dusted with dried fawn tears, garnished with carefully selected miniature radishes gently cut to resemble a rose of Sharon in full bloom.

How can we ever know what he masticated upon?

Oh, wait. Maybe the Bible documented what he ate?

Let us now turn to the holy text to see, shall we?

> 1 Now it happened that while the crowd was pressing
> around Him and listening to the word of God, He was
> standing by the lake of Gennesaret; 2 and He saw two
> boats lying at the edge of the lake; but the fishermen
> had gotten out of them and were washing their nets.
> 3 And He got into one of the boats, which was Simon's
> and asked him to put out a little way from the land.
> And He sat down and [began] teaching the people
> from the boat. 4 When He had finished speaking, He
> said to Simon, "Put out into the deep water and let

> down your nets for a catch." 5 Simon answered and
> said, "Master, we worked hard all night and caught
> nothing, but I will do as You say [and] let down the
> nets." 6 When they had done this, they enclosed a
> great quantity of fish, and their nets [began] to break;
> 7 so they signaled to their partners in the other boat
> for them to come and help them. And they came and
> filled both of the boats, so that they began to sink.
>
> 8 But when Simon Peter saw [that], he fell down at
> Jesus' feet, saying, "Go away from me Lord, for I am a
> sinful man, O Lord!" 9 For amazement had seized him
> and all his companions because of the catch of fish
> which they had taken; 10 and so also [were] James
> and John, sons of Zebedee, who were partners with
> Simon. And Jesus said to Simon, "Do not fear, from
> now on you will be catching men." 11 When they had
> brought their boats to land, they left everything and
> followed Him.
>
> – Luke 5:1-11

Maybe that's a bad proof text for meat consumption because that passage didn't explicitly say that Jesus and the boys ate the fish, but I'm guessing they did. It's not like they had koi ponds to stock back then.

Now, I'll give it to you that this episode from Luke's laptop didn't directly state that they morphed the yellow fin into a mess of sushi, but it did shoot down any and all notions that Jesus was anti-fishing because he enabled his disciples to catch (read: kill) so many fish that their nets were about to break and their boat was about to sink.

By the way, that's called a good day on the water where I come from.

Here's a question for those who hold that killing animals and/or fish for any reason is naughty: Did we just read that Jesus aided and abetted the seizure of fish?

The answer would be ... yes.

In addition, I'm sure some sage naysayer is queuing up with the quip/query, "Did Jesus really have to slaughter so many fishies?" "Isn't that overkill?" "Isn't JC being greedy?"

I'm sure Alicia Silverstone would think that if she read what Jesus did in the aforementioned Scriptures, she'd probably think Jesus wasn't acting very Christ-like. Shame on Jesus.

For fun, lets say the anti-hunting/fishing folks are spot on in their assessment of the sin of hunting and fishing.

What if Jesus' assisting of his disciples in the catching and killing of so many fish was immoral?

What are the implications if, indeed, Christ erred by committing the two-fold sin of "greedy fishing"?

The simple answer is that, if fishing is a sin and Jesus encouraged and enabled his boys to do it in such a vainglorious fashion, then from a salvation standpoint we've got a problem, because in order for Jesus to make an atonement for anyone's sins, according to the Bible, he had to be perfect; and according to your anti-fishing and hunting blather, Christ just blew it big time; and that means we're all screwed and his sacrifice meant *nada*, being stained by the peccadillo of catching a cluster of perch.

Therefore, my anti-meat-eating brethren, he couldn't be God, according to you, the tree-humpers, because he violated, on a mega-scale, the fishes' "animal rights"; and the God they've made up in their whirring tin brain would never ever endorse such an activity.

Indeed, if they're right and the Son of God did transgress by the catching, killing, skinning and eating of fish fillets, then we're all doomed. That is, unless of course, they're wrong. And the Jesus they worship is a figment of their fetid, protein-deficient imagination.

Heretofore, we've been provided with biblical proof that, according to Dr. Luke, Jesus blessed his boys with amazing fishing advice that enabled them to waylay massive amounts of fish; but it didn't say they ate them. So, in order to assuage the doubts of the fastidious, let's plow on to see if and when Hey-Soos dined on fish meat.

> 33 The people saw them going, and many
> recognized them and ran there together on foot from
> all the cities, and got there ahead of them. 34 When
> Jesus went ashore, He saw a large crowd, and He felt
> compassion for them because they were like sheep
> without a shepherd; and He began to teach them many
> things. 35 When it was already quite late, His disciples
> came to Him and said, "This place is desolate and it
> is already quite late; 36 send them away so that they
> may go into the surrounding countryside and villages
> and buy themselves something to eat." 37 But He
> answered them, "You give them something to eat!"

> And they said to Him, "Shall we go and spend two hundred denarii on bread and give them something to eat?" 38 And He said to them, "How many loaves do you have? Go look!" And when they found out, they said, "Five, and two fish." 39 And He commanded them all to sit down by groups on the green grass. 40 They sat down in groups of hundreds and of fifties. 41 And He took the five loaves and the two fish, and looking up toward heaven, He blessed the food and broke the loaves and He kept giving them to the disciples to set before them; and He divided up the two fish among them all. 42 They all ate and were satisfied, 43 and they picked up twelve full baskets of the broken pieces, and also of the fish. 44There were five thousand men who ate the loaves. – Mark 6:33-44

Okay let's break this bad boy down:

- Jesus has a lot of lost people around him.
- He begins to teach them 'til it got late.
- The folks are getting hungry. (Hungry Christians get mean, gotta feed 'em.)
- His disciples said to get rid of them.
- Jesus is like, "You feed them."
- His disciples are like, "Yeah, right."
- Then Jesus taps their food source, which totaled five loaves of bread and two fish.
- Jesus had 'em sit down, took the bread and fish, looked up

> to heaven, blessed the food and then, miraculously, they all ate and were satisfied.

Please note that it clearly states that they all ate fish.

Everyone. Including Jesus. Ate fish.

They didn't just feed on the miraculous Wonder Bread, but also the fish. The fish that someone caught and killed, which Christ blessed and multiplied.

Did that hurt, anti-flesh eaters? Should I call a wambulence?

Jesus is clearly cool with meat consumption. I'm talkin' mass scale, miracle meat consumption; which according to my good buddy and master chef, Bob Corcorran, owner of River Smith's restaurant, would be over a ton of fish to feed those hungry mouths.

What's also interesting about the feeding of the 5000 from John's take on the event is that supernatural multiplication of fish flesh was a sign to the folks that Jesus was "The Prophet" sent by God (Jn 6:1-14).

Yep, the proliferation of fish fillets equated to a divine attestation to those lucky enough to watch that phenomenon go down. They sure as shizzle didn't see it as a sin. Oh, no. On the contrary, they saw that paranormal provision of meat as proof that Jesus was sent from Jehovah. Boom.

I know, some folks are probably thinking, "Okay, smart guy. Jesus enabled his disciples to slay and eat fish. Big whoop. A lot of vegetarians are cool with eating fish. However, both quoted chapters said squat about Jesus' eating actual *meat* meat."

You're right. You got me. It said fish and not beef or veal. I'm so busted.

Even though I still don't get how the anti-hunters and anti-meat-eaters make a distinction between slaughtering a pretty fish and grubbing it being okay, while shooting, killing and eating a four legged animal is not but ... whatever.

I guess I lose. You guys win. I'm such a dork.

Oh, wait. I forgot about the Passover. You remember, the famous Last Supper?

> 12 On the first day of Unleavened Bread, when the
> Passover [lamb] was being sacrificed, His
> disciples said to Him, "Where do You want us to
> go and prepare for You to eat the Passover?" 13 And
> He sent two of His disciples and said to them, «Go into
> the city, and a man will meet you carrying a pitcher of
> water; follow him; 14 and wherever he enters, say to
> the owner of the house, 'The Teacher says, "Where is
> My guest room in which I may eat the Passover with
> My disciples?"' 15 "And he himself will show you a
> large upper room furnished [and] ready; prepare for
> us there." 16 The disciples went out and came to the
> city, and found [it] just as He had told them; and they
> prepared the Passover.
>
> 17 When it was evening He came with the
> twelve. 18 As they were reclining [at the table] and
> eating, Jesus said, "Truly I say to you that one of you
> will betray Me-- one who is eating with Me."
>
> – Mark 14:12-18

RISE, KILL & EAT

Looks like I'm back on top.

Let's recap, shall we?

The Passover, a holy event, entailed the slaughter of a lamb. Not only did they kill that little bugger, they also grilled it and ate it.

Please note, in v.14 Jesus said he's going to eat it, the lamb, with his disciples; and again in v.18, Jesus said "the one who betrays me is eating with me."

It's pretty clear to this redneck that Jesus not only was cool with consuming fish, but he also was down with meat consumption, so much so that it was his last meal. Before his execution, Jesus loved him some tasty lamb chops, thereby blowing all to hell the vegans' being able to use Jesus as an example of vegetable quiche eating only.

One more note of importance, y'know, just to rub it in, that Jesus was no vegan.

In John chapter twenty-one, in his post-resurrection, pre-ascension person, Jesus proved to his doubting disciples that he was the risen Christ, not by hugging them and singing to them "Friends are Friends Forever When the Lord's the Lord of Them", but by allowing them to catch 153 humongous fish and then personally grilling the fish and eating them with his boys.

Check it out: the catching and killing of another, mind-blowing haul of fish, and then cooking and consuming their succulent flesh, was all the proof his disciples needed to know that *that* man on the beach was no normal man, but the risen Son of God.

Finally, in probably one of the most amazing stories of redemption that Jesus every parlayed on the public's noggin was the parable of the prodigal son.

> It's pretty clear to this redneck that Jesus not only was cool with consuming fish, but he also was down with meat consumption, so much so that it was his last meal. Before his execution, Jesus loved him some tasty lamb chops, thereby blowing all to hell the vegans' being able to use Jesus as an example of vegetable quiche eating only.

> 11 And He said, "A
> man had two sons. 12
> The younger of
> them said to his
> father, 'Father, give me
> the share of the
> estate that falls to
> me.' So he divided his
> wealth between them. 13 And not many days later, the
> younger son gathered everything together and went
> on a journey into a distant country, and there he
> squandered his estate with loose living. 14 Now when
> he had spent everything, a severe famine occurred in
> that country, and he began to be impoverished. 15
> So he went and hired himself out to one of the
> citizens of that country, and he sent him into
> his fields to feed swine. 16 And he would have
> gladly filled his stomach with the pods that the
> swine were eating, and no one was giving [anything]
> to him. 17 But when he came to his senses, he
> said, 'How many of my father's hired men have
> more than enough bread, but I am dying here with
> hunger! 18 I will get up and go to my father, and will
> say to him, "Father, I have sinned against heaven, and

> in your sight; 19 I am no longer worthy to be
> called your son; make me as one of your hired
> men.’” 20 So he got up and came to his father. But
> while he was still a long way off, his father saw him and
> felt compassion [for him], and ran and embraced him
> and kissed him. 21 And the son said to him, ‘Father, I
> have sinned against heaven and in your sight; I
> am no longer worthy to be called your son.’ 22
> But the father said to his slaves, ‘Quickly bring out
> the best robe and put it on him, and put a ring on
> his hand and sandals on his feet; 23and bring the
> fattened calf, kill it, and let us eat and celebrate; 24
> for this son of mine was dead and has come to life
> again; he was lost and has been found.’ And they
> began to celebrate.” – Luke 15: 11-24

In this familiar narrative, we have a rich look inside the father’s heart towards lost causes who’re squandering their lives away on vice.

Dudes like yours truly, thirty years after my conversion, still gets misty-eyed thinking that, after all the dastardly stuff I’ve done, and how I ruined my life, other people’s lives and rebelled against a loving God, as soon as I came to my senses, the father was always there, ready, waiting and willing, no … running to my rescue.

And check this out: In one of the most stunning stories of redemption, reconciliation and restoration there’s a big ol’ Texas BBQ in the big middle of it.

Yep, the father showed his joy, love and acceptance by giving his repentant boy a nice ring, a wardrobe upgrade, some killer sandals and then ordering his posse to kill and grill their fattened calf.

Pretty telling what the Bible thinks about eating meat, that in one of its most touching tales of salvation it entails the father (God) ordering a massive meat platter to celebrate this son who was once lost, but now is found.

And lastly, for the coup de grace, the end all to being able to use Jesus as an anti-meat-killing/eating hippie, I offer you Mark 7:14-15, 17-19:

> 14 Again Jesus called the crowd to him and said,
> "Listen to me, everyone, and understand this. 15
> Nothing outside a person can defile them by going into
> them. Rather, it is what comes out of a person that
> defiles them." … 17 After he had left the crowd and
> entered the house, his disciples asked him about this
> parable. 18 "Are you so dull?" he asked. "Don't you
> see that nothing that enters a person from the outside
> can defile them? 19 For it doesn't go into their heart
> but into their stomach, and then out of the body." (In
> saying this, Jesus declared all foods clean.)

So, in conclusion, I guess Jesus is okay with eating fish and meat. Which means you're out in left field trying to pitch Jesus Christ as a crouton eater only. Boo-Frickety-Hoo.

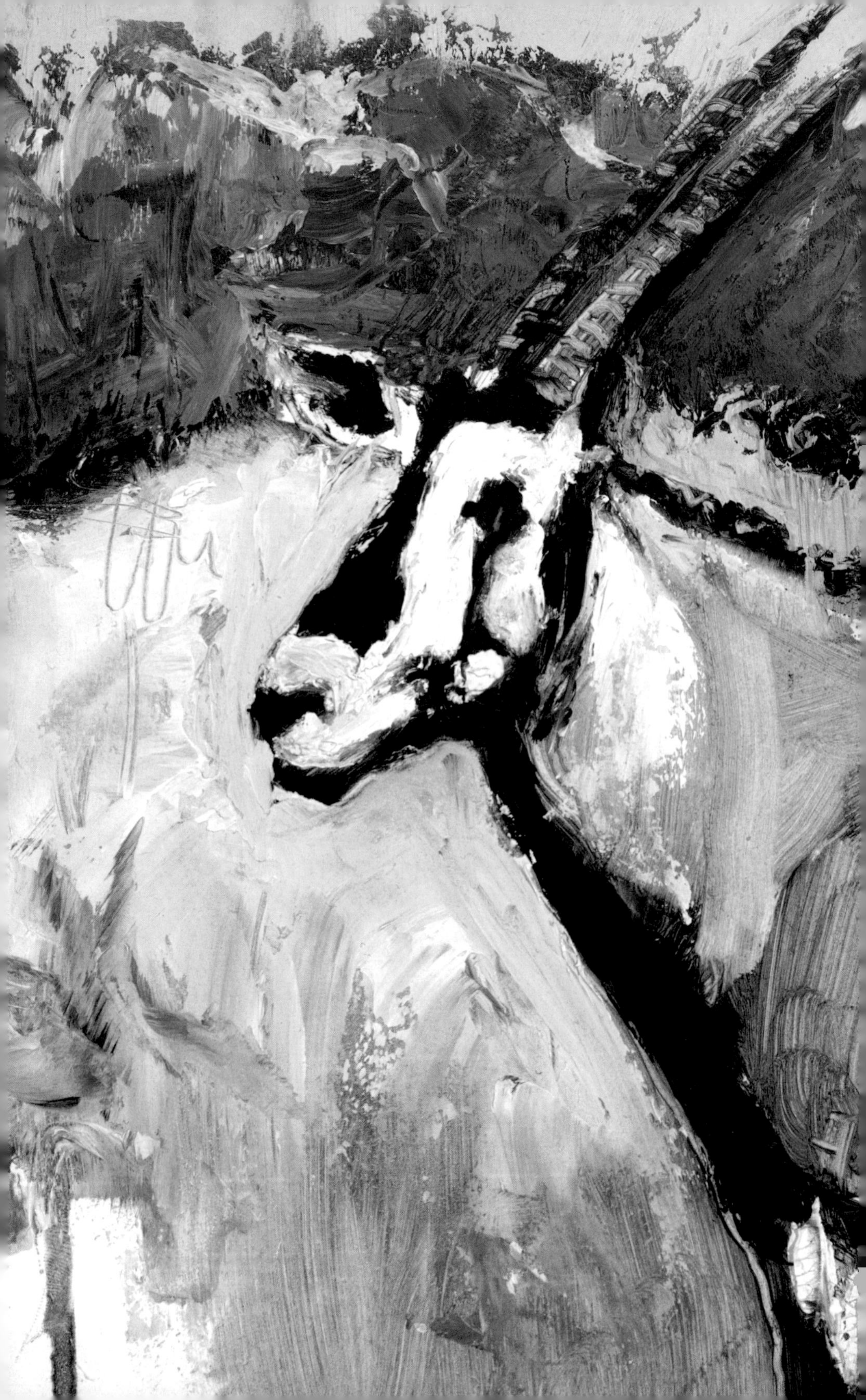

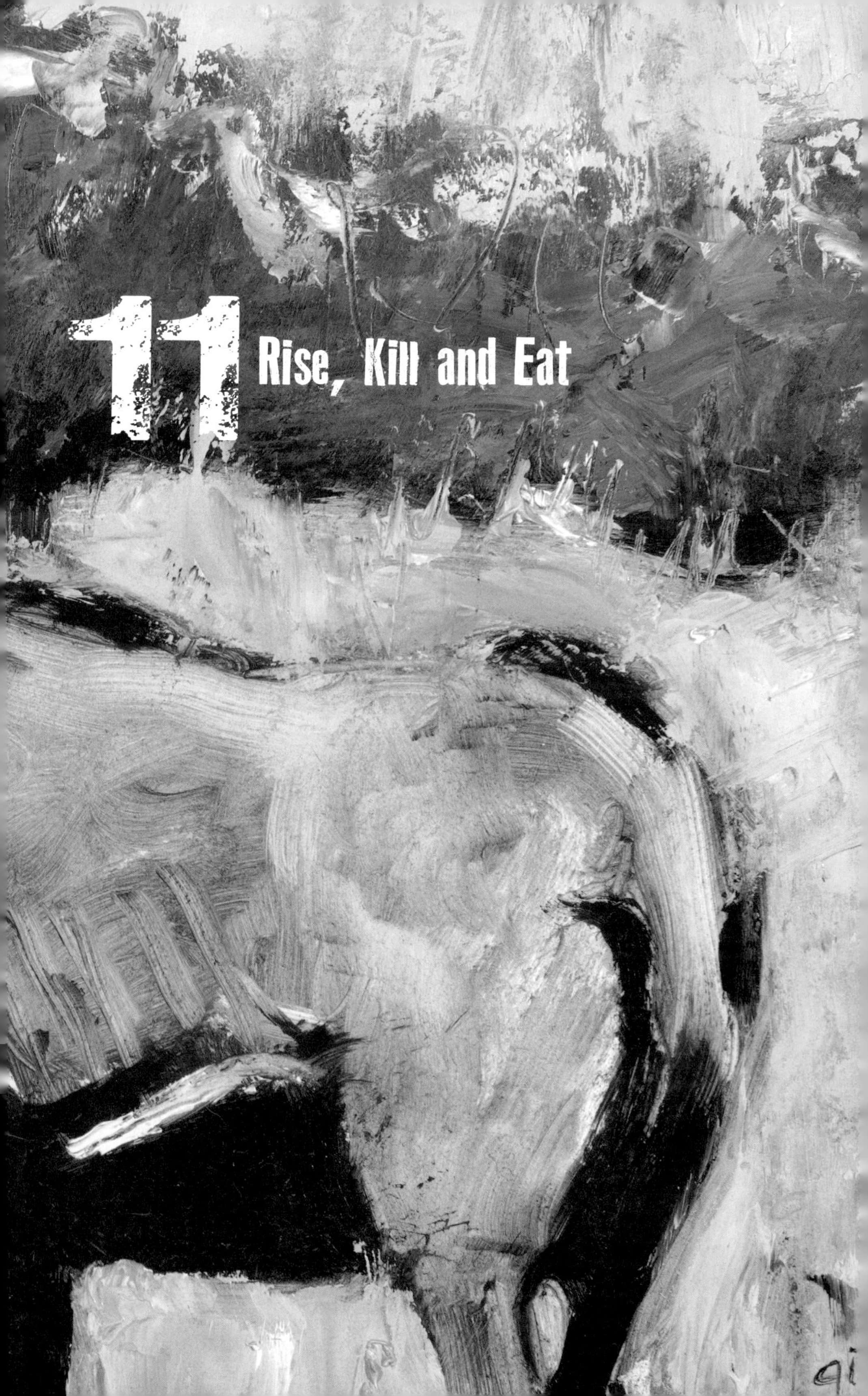

11 Rise, Kill and Eat

giles
7/08

Rise, Kill and Eat

Christians can be knuckleheads. Unfortunately, we still do stupid crap just like the unwashed cattle that do not profess a knowledge of God.

At least I do.

I know some of you angels live a perfect life, but not me, sister.

Indeed, after thirty years of trying to follow Jesus' lead, unfortunately, I still get wrapped around the axle saying, doing or believing something that's straight up goofy, of which I have to be corrected by the word of God and by the few friends who still care enough about me to rebuke me.

I wish I was perfect, but I've gotta die to be made truly whole and that hasn't happened yet. So as long as this earth suit encumbers me I'm going to be making mistakes and needing grace. As Uncle Si would say, "That's a fact, Jack." It's a biblical reality, in all its glory, in this fallen world.

The cool thing is, however, that it's just not me that's been a dorky, God-loving, yet sinful doofus. The Bible is replete with faith-filled characters that practiced and believed things, for a time, which would make Saturday Night Live's "Church Lady" spit her sweet tea across her parlor.

One of my favorite characters who gives me great hope when I make grave mistakes is Jesus's disciple named Peter.

Peter was the disciple with the foot shaped mouth. For those hip to the New Testament, you know that Peter ran hot and cold in his devotion to Jesus and the gospel. He swung like a violent pendulum, at times boldly declaring his allegiance to Jesus and then, one hour later, cussing up a storm denying he ever knew him.

In addition, to Peter's bold confession and his equally brash denial of Jesus, he also got a bubble-off-level with the heart of the gospel message, which is encapsulated nicely by the Apostle Paul in Ephesians 2:8, 9: "For by grace you have been saved through faith; and that not of yourselves, it is the gift of God; 9 not as a result of works, so that no one may boast."

Peter also lost focus that, "For God so loved the world, that He gave His only begotten Son, that whoever believes in Him shall not perish, but have eternal life."

Peter, a Jew, believed that God so loved the Jews but he just kind of liked the Gentiles. Yep, old thickheaded Pete got swept up with the first century Judaizers that had infiltrated the church and were putting forth the heresy that believing wasn't good enough, and that to be truly pleasing to God you had to have your penis circumcised (see Galatians 2).

Indeed, Mr. "Saved by Grace" turned into Mr. "Saved by Grace plus you got get your rumpled foreskin removed from your one-eyed monster". (Isn't there a German fairy tale named, Rumpledforeskin?) Anyway, Peter drifted from the heart of the gospel preaching circumcision while avoiding the Gentiles like

Rise, Kill and Eat

Rosie O'Donnell does low-fat yogurt.

So, God, being faithful to his wayward disciple, would either rebuke him via a non-discombobulated apostle or, as in this occasion, he had to put him into a trance and give him a vision just so he would preach grace alone to someone who wasn't Jewish and who hadn't had his banana cut.

Now, if you were God, and you wanted to expand the mind of a prejudiced religious person who's theologically out in left field to embrace God's love for people not of their particular stripe, what kind of illustration would you utilize to get your point across to Mr. "Forgetful that God loves folks other than the Jews, irrespective of whether or not they've had their Johnson snipped"?

Would you use a hunting illustration? I doubt it. But God did.

Check it out ...

Acts 10

> 1 There was a certain man in Caesarea called Cornelius,
> a centurion of the band called the Italian band, 2 A
> devout man, and one that feared God with all his
> house, which gave much alms to the people, and
> prayed to God alway. 3 He saw in a vision evidently
> about the ninth hour of the day an angel of God
> coming in to him, and saying unto him, Cornelius. 4
> And when he looked on him, he was afraid, and said,
> What is it, Lord? And he said unto him, Thy prayers and
> thine alms are come up for a memorial before God. 5
> And now send men to Joppa, and call for one Simon,
> whose surname is Peter: 6 He lodgeth with one Simon

a tanner, whose house is by the sea side: he shall tell
thee what thou oughtest to do. 7 And when the angel
which spake unto Cornelius was departed, he called
two of his household servants, and a devout soldier of
them that waited on him continually; 8 And when he
had declared all these things unto them, he sent them
to Joppa.

9 On the morrow, as they went on their journey,
and drew nigh unto the city, Peter went up upon
the housetop to pray about the sixth hour: 10 And
he became very hungry, and would have eaten: but
while they made ready, he fell into a trance, 11 And
saw heaven opened, and a certain vessel descending
unto him, as it had been a great sheet knit at the four
corners, and let down to the earth: 12 Wherein were
all manner of fourfooted beasts of the earth, and wild
beasts, and creeping things, and fowls of the air. 13
And there came a voice to him, Rise, Peter; kill, and
eat. 14 But Peter said, Not so, Lord; for I have never
eaten any thing that is common or unclean. 15 And the
voice spake unto him again the second time, What God
hath cleansed, that call not thou common. 16 This was
done thrice: and the vessel was received up again into
heaven.

17 Now while Peter doubted in himself what this vision
which he had seen should mean, behold, the men
which were sent from Cornelius had made inquiry for
Simon's house, and stood before the gate, 18 And
called, and asked whether Simon, which was surnamed
Peter, were lodged there. 19 While Peter thought on

the vision, the Spirit said unto him, Behold, three men
seek thee. 20 Arise therefore, and get thee down,
and go with them, doubting nothing: for I have sent
them. 21 Then Peter went down to the men which
were sent unto him from Cornelius; and said, Behold, I
am he whom ye seek: what is the cause wherefore ye
are come? 22 And they said, Cornelius the centurion, a
just man, and one that feareth God, and of good report
among all the nation of the Jews, was warned from
God by an holy angel to send for thee into his house,
and to hear words of thee. 23 Then called he them
in, and lodged them. And on the morrow Peter went
away with them, and certain brethren from Joppa
accompanied him.

24 And the morrow after they entered into Caesarea.
And Cornelius waited for them, and had called
together his kinsmen and near friends. 25 And as Peter
was coming in, Cornelius met him, and fell down at his
feet, and worshipped him. 26 But Peter took him up,
saying, Stand up; I myself also am a man. 27 And as he
talked with him, he went in, and found many that were
come together. 28 And he said unto them, Ye know
how that it is an unlawful thing for a man that is a Jew
to keep company, or come unto one of another nation;
but God hath shewed me that I should not call any
man common or unclean. 29 Therefore came I unto
you without gainsaying, as soon as I was sent for: I ask
therefore for what intent ye have sent for me?

30 And Cornelius said, Four days ago I was fasting
until this hour; and at the ninth hour I prayed in my

house, and, behold, a man stood before me in bright clothing, 31 And said, Cornelius, thy prayer is heard, and thine alms are had in remembrance in the sight of God. 32 Send therefore to Joppa, and call hither Simon, whose surname is Peter; he is lodged in the house of one Simon a tanner by the seaside: who, when he cometh, shall speak unto thee. 33 Immediately therefore I sent to thee; and thou hast well done that thou art come. Now therefore are we all here present before God, to hear all things that are commanded thee of God.

34 Then Peter opened his mouth, and said, Of a truth I perceive that God is no respecter of persons: 35 But in every nation he that feareth him, and worketh righteousness, is accepted with him. 36 The word which God sent unto the children of Israel, preaching peace by Jesus Christ: (he is Lord of all:) 37 That word, I say, ye know, which was published throughout all Judaea, and began from Galilee, after the baptism which John preached; 38 How God anointed Jesus of Nazareth with the Holy Ghost and with power: who went about doing good, and healing all that were oppressed of the devil; for God was with him. 39 And we are witnesses of all things which he did both in the land of the Jews, and in Jerusalem; whom they slew and hanged on a tree: 40 Him God raised up the third day, and shewed him openly; 41 Not to all the people, but unto witnesses chosen before of God, even to us, who did eat and drink with him after he rose from the dead. 42 And he commanded us to preach unto the

> people, and to testify that it is he which was ordained
> of God to be the Judge of quick and dead. 43 To him
> give all the prophets witness, that through his name
> whosoever believeth in him shall receive remission of
> sins.
>
> 44 While Peter yet spake these words, the Holy Ghost
> fell on all them which heard the word. 45 And they of
> the circumcision which believed were astonished, as
> many as came with Peter, because that on the Gentiles
> also was poured out the gift of the Holy Ghost. 46 For
> they heard them speak with tongues, and magnify
> God. Then answered Peter, 47 Can any man forbid
> water, that these should not be baptized, which have
> received the Holy Ghost as well as we? 48 And he
> commanded them to be baptized in the name of the
> Lord. Then prayed they him to tarry certain days.

Let’s recap, shall we?

In order for Peter to preach to this non-Jewish, God-hungry fellow named Cornelius, God had to put Pete into a trance and give him a heavenly vision that represented the Gospel via hunting illustration.

In cased you skipped over that big chunk of Scripture here’s the vision part again …

> 9 On the morrow, as they went on their journey,
> and drew nigh unto the city, Peter went up upon
> the housetop to pray about the sixth hour: 10 And
> he became very hungry, and would have eaten: but
> while they made ready, he fell into a trance, 11 And
> saw heaven opened, and a certain vessel descending

> unto him, as it had been a great sheet knit at the four
> corners, and let down to the earth: 12 Wherein were
> all manner of fourfooted beasts of the earth, and wild
> beasts, and creeping things, and fowls of the air. 13
> And there came a voice to him, Rise, Peter; kill, and
> eat. 14 But Peter said, Not so, Lord; for I have never
> eaten any thing that is common or unclean. 15 And the
> voice spake unto him again the second time, What God
> hath cleansed, that call not thou common. 16 This was
> done thrice: and the vessel was received up again into
> heaven.

This is interesting.

For God to get the gospel message through to old cement head Peter, he showed him a slew of animals, domesticated and wild; plus creepy things and all kinds of birds of which some, according to levitical law, obviously were forbidden; and he told Peter to rise, kill them and eat them. Peter, gets all high and mighty and says, "No way, God, I don't eat what's unclean." And God's like, "Uh … excuse me, but what I have cleansed don't you call it unclean." Peter, being the stubborn monkey that he was, had to have this vision/lesson showed to him three times before he got the message not to treat non-Jews like they're a Rottweiler with rabies.

Pretty amazing, eh, that God would utilize a hunting illustration to get across the greatest story ever told to his confused disciple.

Go figure that the most powerful message of grace and acceptance was communicated by a hunting visual.

Of Mice and Men

12 Of Mice and Men

The Bible is crystal clear that there is a big, whopping, distinction between man and animals, although I'll grant you sometimes men act like animals and vice versa. (Gen..1:20-28; Ps.50:10,11; Jer.27:5; 1Cor.10:25,26)

Oh, BTW, every time men acted like an animal, God didn't praise them but condemned them because, hello, God expects more from men than monkeys because men, not animals, were created in his image and are commanded to follow his ways. (Job 35:10,11; Ps.32:9; Ps.73:22; Prov.26:3; Eccl.12:13,14; Mt.28:18-20; Heb.9:27)

Oh, and one more BTW, Jesus died to save men not animals. Just an FYI, in case you were muddy on that issue. (Isa.53:5,8; Rom.5:12-19; 1Tim.2:4-6)

Look, both men and animals were created by God and are his, but he gave the stewardship role over the created order to men not raccoons. Can you imagine if raccoons ran everything? This place would be more jacked up than the United States under Obama's care, maybe.

Now, just because man has dominion over the critters doesn't mean he's to abuse them. The Scripture's replete with instructions regarding how mankind is to care for the planet's four-footed, feathered and finny friends.

That said, there's an allotment for the domestication of animals and the hunting of animals and the Bible is chock-full of holy folks that owned livestock, fished and hunted and made clothing out of their hides; and there's not one gnarly passage that condemns any of the aforementioned. (Exo.21:28,29; Dt.22:1-4; 1Sam.12:3; Job 1:3; Isa.1:3; Lk.10:34; Lk.19:30-35; Jn.10:1-14)

The abuses of the created order comes when men detach themselves from the Scriptural edicts of the proper treatment of the earth and its natural resources and not when it attaches itself to the dictates of the *Verbum Dei*.

Afterburner:
The Top Reasons Why I Love Hunting

Afterburner:
The Top Ten Reasons Why I Love Hunting

Herewith are ten reasons why I dig hunting . . .

10. When I'm out hunting, the locations are usually so remote that my necessary evil, i.e. cell phone and my buddies' cell phones, do not work and thus, depending on the length of the hunt, I have a 3-14 day timeframe to be left the heck alone. Thank you, Jesus. No doubt some of you are thinking, "I can't live, if living is without you" in relation to your electronic appendage. Trust me, you'll survive, and believe it or not — and this might hurt some of you egoists — the world will continue to turn without your input.

9. Our sport is 99.9% devoid of nasty, whiny, man-hating, stretch-pants-wearing, mullet-sporting, anti-American, nerve-grating feminists and nutty liberals. Yep, around the campfire and in the field, the lunatic left's yarbling is nonexistent. Why the absence of the left's asininity out in the brush? The answer is simple: The tree humpers don't hunt, which is awesome! For my God and country-loving tribe, this makes the air smell fresher, the food taste better, the wine taste sweeter, the buzz last longer, the stars shine brighter, the voice of God clearer, and the trip overwhelmingly blissful with such jackanapes missing from our mix. Yep, the hunting camp is a traditional values paradise.

8. Less noise. One of the things I hate about city life is the noise. Daily I find myself walking around yelling like Yosemite Sam, "I hate noise ... can't stand noise . . . Noise . . . Noise . . . noise!", which inadvertently adds to the racket, which explains much of my life. Where I live (Miami) everything is frickin' noisy. Horns honkin', people yelling on their cell phones, folks fighting, screaming and complaining in English, Spanish, Russian, Portuguese and Yiddish — and that's just in the foyer of our church. (By the way, can Starbucks get a coffee steamer that doesn't sound like a wild boar being gutted with a dull chainsaw? Is that too much to ask?) Out in the field and away from the concrete, the hunter enjoys the magical perk of peace and quiet.

7. Art by God. The hunter gets an ocular overload, as he is fortunate to behold the handiwork of the Creator in an intimate and intimidating way. Yes, away from the man-made stercore tauri one gets to behold the Designer showing off his flora and fauna in a funkalicious fashion. Explosive colors, an endless variety of birds, animals, fish, reptiles, freaky insects, threatening mountains, trickling and raging rivers, and brilliant stars are the canvas God rolls out and slaps the on looking hunter with. I know this will upset some indoor Nancy-boy pastors, but I get more God out of nature than I do your dull church service. The hunter understands what King David meant in Psalm 23 when he says that God "makes me lie down in green pastures, he leads me beside quiet waters, he restores my soul." Call me crazy, but God's art crushes any Abstract/Modern art which usually looks like someone wiped their butt on a piece of paper, framed it and called it good.

6. Hunting revives the hunter's primal roots. Just getting out in the wild reconnects me with my original spiritual and physical moorings. When God created Adam and Eve, He made certain that their initial crib didn't have cable TV or a home association. Yep, God didn't want His kids' first experiences to be lame and tame. Adam and Eve were made to be wild, not mild, and were purposely crafted to interface 24/7 with wild beasts. Lucky bastards.

Non-hunter: If you or your kids are screwed up, one of the many reasons could be that you have separated yourself and your brood from what they need, namely regular doses of the irregular wild. Try it. It's magical. There is something that the undomesticated does to a person that no Lysol-disinfected, five star hotel on South Beach, slow cruise to Nassau, or a 3-day hell trip to Disneyland could provide — and the hunter is stubbornly locked onto this fact. Yes, you can go to Disneyland, and we'll go to Africa or Texas or Maine or Alaska.

The hunt causes one's senses to come alive, and as a result, they're taken to a higher level by simply pursuing the prey. Yes, the eyes, ears, nose, feet and hands kick into high gear like they don't when you're standing in the snaking stooge line at McDonald's waiting for their new McCrap sandwich before you return to your office cubicle to inhale the stale, fart-laden, recirculated office "air."

5. Hunting takes the funk out of dysfunctional families. What I've seen in 30 plus years out in the hunting fields is this: The family that hunts together stays together. Hunting requires communication between the hunting parties. Most families communicate with each other about as often as Bill has sex

with Hillary. Hunting cures this (the communication part, not the Bill and Hillary stuff).

There's a lot that goes into being a successful hunter, and it demands plenty of quality time spent between the tribe discussing safety, terrain, conservation, the particular animals to be pursued, and choices of weapons, boots, clothes, bullets, bows/arrows . . . you get the point, don't 'cha? After all the aforementioned prelim stuff is done with, then the hunt commences, which includes sitting, walking, stalking, and then relaxing around the sacred campfire, where it's just you guys talking, laughing and anticipating the next day, and — excuse my redundancy — you are all together. The hunter understands this: Family is everything, all else is BS.

4. Hunting provides veggies for the vegans. I love the fact that the PETA vegans couldn't eat their sassy salad or their edamame burger if it weren't for the blistering fact that farmers/hunters have to shoot animals so that the vapid vegan can smugly eat his garbanzo bean patty. Earth to PETA: Animals prey on your in-demand, non-animal grub — and the farmers don't like it, and they shoot them. Do you need a tissue?

Yes, the "save the animal" dipsticks who don't eat meat wouldn't have their holy lettuce if it were not for farmers shooting PETA's "friends" like the rabbits, deer, wild hogs and other critters that decimate the vegetarians' victuals. However, I wouldn't let it bug you now, PETA. Before you eat your salad, just smoke another doobie and forget about the fact that for you to have your cute little baby carrot, it entailed a farmer putting the bam to Bambi. Oh, the irony.

3. Hunting provides massive amounts of food for the poor. Unlike the liberal blowhards who talk about helping the poor, many hunters practically do it by feeding them. The hunter, who generally speaking, is a conservative, is supposed to be, according to the Mange Stream Media, a calloused living heart donor. However, the reality is that we provide a massive, benevolent source of high-protein, low-fat food to the poor at our own expense. Put that in your hookah and smoke it, morons.

Here's the truth, weepy, "save the poor" hypocrites: The "evil" group known to you as hunters gives away hundreds of thousands of pounds of the best meat on the planet at their expense to the poorest among us. In the last couple of years alone, my buddies and I have paid for the hunting, butchering and processing of, conservatively, 10,000 pounds of sweet venison for the poor in Africa and at risk kids, Christian ministries, and abused and battered women here in the U.S of A. That's 10,000 plus pounds of meat just between a few guys in the last few years. How do you, the "loving liberal", stack up against that? Not very well, I'll bet.

2. Hunters put their money where their mouth is. The yarbling libs and PETA are a full-of-sheeta crowd that would love to make us all believe that they are true stewards of nature and that hunters are Agent Orange to animals and land. However, if the truth can still be told, it's the hunter who doles out nearly three hundred million bucks a year in special surtaxes on guns, ammo, camo underwear and other outdoor supplies which go to state conservation programs. The tree humpers don't pay these taxes, girlfriend, the hunters do. The hunters. The hunters. The hunters.

For now, for the brainwashed crowd that's probably enough 411 on how the hunter is the true conservationist who puts his money where his mouth is. Maybe later I'll write about how the hunters' hard earned capital is what saves the swamps, underwrites wildlife research, and has kept many species around the planet from going extinct — not PETA.

1. Hunters are the salt of the earth. Every group has their jerks, and it's true that everybody sucks, but as far as I'm concerned, hunters suck less. Matter of fact, I'd say that 95% of the people I have met in the hallowed hunting camp have been upright, pleasant, courteous, grateful, hard working, God-and-country-loving, family oriented folks with whom it was my deepest pleasure to be able to share a few days pursuing game.

. . . [W]e need to conserve that bitter impulse that we have inherited from primitive man. It alone permits us the greatest luxury of all, the ability to enjoy a vacation from the human condition through an authentic, 'immersion in Nature' ... and this, in turn, can be achieved only by placing himself in relation to another animal. But there is no animal, pure animal, other than a wild one, and the relationship with him is the hunt. –Jose Ortega y Gasset.

About the Author

Doug Giles is the man behind **ClashDaily.com**. In addition to driving ClashDaily.com, Giles is a popular columnist on Townhall.com and the author of the book *Raising Righteous & Rowdy Girls.*

Doug's articles have also appeared on several other print and online news sources, including *The Washington Times, The Daily Caller, Fox Nation, USA Today, The Wall Street Journal, The Washington Examiner, The Blaze, American Hunter Magazine, The Dallas Safari Club* and *ABC News.*

He's been a frequent guest on the *Fox News Channel* and *Fox Business Channel* as well as many nationally syndicated radio shows across the nation.

Giles and his wife Margaret have two daughters: Hannah, who devastated ACORN with her 2009 nation shaking undercover videos, and Regis who is an NRA columnist, huntress and Second Amendment activist.

DG's interests include guns, big game hunting, big game fishing, fine art, cigars, helping wounded warriors, and being a big pain in the butt to people who dislike God and the USA.

Accolades for Giles and ClashDaily.com include …

- Liberty Alliance LLC ranked #1 among conservative media companies on the Inc 500/5000 list for 2013
- One of "The 40 Best Conservative Websites Of 2013"
- Giles was recognized as one of "The 50 Best Conservative Columnists Of 2013"
- ClashDaily.com was recognized as one of "The 100 Most Popular Conservative Websites For 2013"
- Doug was noted as "Hot Conservative New Media Superman" By Politichicks

Speaking Engagements

Doug Giles speaks to college, business, community, church, advocacy and men's groups throughout the United States and internationally. His expertise includes issues of Christianity and culture, masculinity vs. metrosexuality, big game hunting and fishing, raising righteous kids in a rank culture, the Second Amendment, personal empowerment, politics, and social change.